Understanding
BIBLE
PROPHECY
for Yourself

Tim LaHaye

HARVEST HOUSE PUBLISHERS
Eugene, Oregon 97402

Cover by Terry Dugan Design, Minneapolis, Minnesota

Published in association with the literary agency of Alive Communications, Inc., 7680 Goddard Street, Suite 200, Colorado Springs, CO 80920

UNDERSTANDING BIBLE PROPHECY FOR YOURSELF
Copyright © 1998, 2001 by Tim LaHaye
Published by Harvest House Publishers
Eugene, Oregon 97402

Library of Congress Cataloging-in-Publication Data
LaHaye, Tim F.
    [How to study Bible prophecy for yourself]
    Understanding Bible Prophecy for Yourself / Tim LaHaye.
        p. cm.—(Tim LaHaye prophecy library)
    Originally published: How to study Bible prophecy for yourself. ©1990.
    ISBN 0-7369-0822-6 (Softcover)
    ISBN 0-7369-0970-2 (Hardcover)
        1. Bible—Prophecies.   2. Bible—Study and teaching.   I. Title.

BS647.3.L34 2002
22.1'5'071—dc21
                                                                        2001038511

Printed in the United States of America.

    02   03   04   05   06   07   / ML DC-VS /   10   9   8   7   6   5   4   3   2   1

*Dedicated to
the memory of Margaret LaHaye,
Bible student, soulwinner,
Child Evangelism director in
Lansing, Michigan, for 23 years,
and my mother.*

*Her love for Bible prophecy
sparked my own. She is now
with her Lord and now
all her questions
are answered, for she "knows
even as she is known."*

CONTENTS

The Urgency 7

1. A New Way to Study Prophecy 11

2. Why Christians Should Study Prophecy 15

3. The Certainty of Christ's Second Coming 23

4. Two Second Comings or One? 31

5. The Tribulation That Separates the Phases 49

6. The Tribulation, the Heart of the Book of Revelation 57

7. The Rapture Before the Tribulation? 77

8. The Church Is Distinct from Israel 83

9. Christians Will Be Saved from the Wrath 89

10. Not Really So Obscure 93

11. Our Lord's Outline of Prophecy 105

12. The Glorious Appearing 119

13. The Christian Resurrection from the Dead 125

14. When Resurrected Christians Meet Their Lord 137

15. The Coming Kingdom of Christ 169

16. Where the Dead Are Now 185

17. The Great White Throne Judgment 199

Drawing Nearer to Christ's Return 215

THE URGENCY

The phenomenal response to the LEFT BEHIND® series of prophetic novels that I coauthored with Jerry B. Jenkins beginning in 1995 has proven people have a deep fascination for knowing about the future. A single book I had hoped would sell 100,000 or so has now become a series with sales of almost 40 million and climbing. The success of the spinoff children's series has already broken all publishing records and proves that the younger generation also yearns to know about the future.

The outrageous terrorist attack on the United States on September 11, 2001 caused prophecy books of all stripes to sell off the charts as people tried to find some insight into the future. Such curiosity, whether fueled by the LEFT BEHIND® series or cataclysmic events, is understandable for man was created by God as an eternal soul, and thus he has always wondered where and how he will spend his enternal future. And apocalyptic-type events such as those that took place in New York City and Washington, D.C. spur millions more people to search for answers.

The good news is that God has given answers to us in His prophetic Word. In fact, 28 percent of the Bible was prophetic when it was first written. In all, there are over 1,000 passages of Scripture that were prophecies at the time they were written, and more than half of them have already been fulfilled. This track record of fulfillment is our assurance that the prophecies not yet ful-filled will come to pass when their time is coming.

I am convinced that their time is rapidly approaching. Of one thing I am certain: There has never been a more urgent time when God's people have needed to know His wonderful plan for the future, and it can be found in the one book that tells us the truth—the Bible.

Our Lord Himself warned His disciples seven times in the Olivet Discourse—which is His description of the end times—that there would be deceivers, false christs, false teachers, and false prophets in the last days. That is an important reason that we as God's people should study the prophetic Word. If we are indeed the generation that is seeing the signs of the times, then we need to know what to expect so that we will not be deceived but will know with certainty God's wonderful plan for the future.

Jesus Christ is coming again! Even many people who are not Christians believe that fact, according to a recent Gallup poll on religion. We can't know the day or the hour (Matthew 25:13), but we can know the season or general period of time. And we should all be prepared for Christ when He comes.

That's what this book is all about—to acquaint you with God's plan for the future so you won't be deceived by false teachers and charlatans who come in sheep's clothing and lead many astray. You will see that the best days for mankind are yet ahead.

Prophecy is not so difficult that we can't understand it, or else God would not have put it into Scripture. This book is written to help you find out for yourself what God has in store for you in both your earthly and your eternal future. You will find it both exciting and inspiring, and I pray that it will motivate you to live every day as if your Lord could return to this earth momentarily as He prom-ised and take you to be with Him, permitting you to become an eyewitness and participant in His exciting plan for the future of mankind.

A special feature of this book is that you will not only *read* about Bible prophecy, but you'll have the opportunity to *study* it as well. This book can help you find out for yourself what prophecy teaches. It is a companion to my other study book by Harvest House Publishers, *How to Study the Bible for Yourself.*

This book is designed to give you a working knowledge of the basics of Bible prophecy and the study of future things. It will equip you to answer the false teachers who are popping up everywhere. Even more important, it will help you straighten out the thinking of the many people you meet who are being deceived by these false teachers.

The Bible challenges us to rightly divide the Word of truth (2 Timothy 2:15). This book will help you rightly divide the truths of prophecy!

1

A NEW WAY TO STUDY PROPHECY

You are about to embark on an exciting but sometimes controversial area of Bible study—one that could change your life. Actually, prophecy sometimes becomes controversial because there are so many different opinions about it. Most of the controversy is over such things as the timing of the Lord's return or the interpretation of signs related to it. Rather than risk being labeled "controversial," some Bible teachers rarely or never teach prophecy, even though it occupies one-third of all Scripture.

A popular Bible teacher taught his congregation the entire New Testament book by book, from Matthew to Jude. After he finished, he started again at the book of Matthew. One of his students interrupted him and said, "You have forgotten the book of Revelation" (an entire book of prophecy). The teacher responded, "Oh, it's too controversial and too difficult to understand."

This is no time in history to avoid "the study of future things," which is what prophecy is. If we avoid teaching Christians the basics about prophecy, they will be "tossed to and fro" by false teachers who come to them with cunningly devised fables and interpretations that will deceive them. And if our expectations are correct, that increase of false teachers has already come on the scene and will continue in the days to come. Christians need to know *more* about prophecy, not less, so that they can be armed with the truth and defend themselves against erroneous teachings.

11

It Is Possible to Understand Bible Prophecy

It is this author's conviction, after studying prophecy for many years, and after writing several books on the subject (including a commentary on the book of Revelation), that prophecy is not so difficult to understand that it should be avoided. Instead, it could be dangerous to the spiritual health of Christians to avoid it. The apostle Paul obviously thought prophecy was important for young Christians to study, for he addressed it in every chapter in the little book of 1 Thessalonians. (Bible scholars tell us that this five-chapter book was probably the very first of his 13 epistles to be written, and that Paul had ministered in Thessalonica for only three weeks, yet obviously had taught many prophetic things during that short time.) In 1 Thessalonians 5:1-5 we read:

> Now, brothers, about times and dates we do not need to write to you, for you know very well that the day of the Lord will come like a thief in the night. While people are saying, "Peace and safety," destruction will come on them suddenly, as labor pains on a pregnant woman, and they will not escape.
>
> But you, brothers, are not in darkness so that this day should surprise you like a thief. You are all sons of the light and sons of the day. We do not belong to the night or to the darkness (NIV).

Obviously Paul did not think that such a subject as "the day of the Lord" (another reference to the second coming of Christ) was too complex for these baby Christians. The fourth chapter of 1 Thessalonians, which we will study later, contains the most detailed description of the coming of Christ for His church to be found in the whole Bible. Then in 2 Thessalonians, which was written just a short time later, Paul taught about the coming of the Antichrist and other future events. Paul clearly did not think that future subjects were too controversial or so hard to understand that they should be ignored. Instead, he considered them important for young believers, and especially essential to challenge Christians to live holy lives in an unholy age.

Some details of prophecy are admittedly difficult to understand, but the essentials are not. And that is why this book is written to help you see by your own study that such subjects as the return of our Lord, the resurrection of the dead, the future activities of the dead (including the judgment seat of Christ for Christians only and the white throne judgment for sinners only), the millennial kingdom, heaven, and the glorious appearing of Christ to rule and reign over this earth are just not that hard to understand.

I am convinced that even if some minor misunderstanding results from the pursuit of prophetic studies, this is still far better than ignoring the subject entirely. Ignorance has never been a virtue! As the apostle Paul said, "I do not want you to be ignorant, brethren" (1 Thessalonians 4:13). I share that concern. I would not have you ignorant about the most important events that God has planned for your future. For if you understand His plan, it will motivate you to live the kind of life that will cause Him to say to you on judgment day, "Well done, good and faithful servant...enter into the joy of your Lord" (Matthew 25:23).

What Makes This Book Different?

Most books on prophecy, including some of mine, are written by one or more authors for the purpose of persuading you of their own interpretation of the prophetic Scriptures. However, the purpose of this book is to help you analyze the prophetic passages of the New Testament (and those from the Old Testament that have a bearing on them) in such a way that you can come to your own conclusions. Scripture texts will be given with space available for you to write your own understanding of the passage. Questions will be asked to help you reach your own conclusions. This way God can speak to you directly on the subject. Then *after* you have reached your own conclusion on what you believe the text teaches, I will provide my understanding of it for comparison. In some cases I will also give other interpretations by Bible-believing Christians for you to consider.

Keep in mind that the Bible was not written to divide Christians, even though it has sometimes been used that way. (In some instances, whole denominations were started over prophetic differences.) The Bible was written to ordinary people like you and me. Most passages are easy to understand and believe if we apply the "golden rule of interpretation" to the passage: *When the plain sense of Scripture makes common sense, seek no other sense, but take every word at its primary, literal meaning, unless the facts of the immediate context clearly indicate otherwise.* As the apostle John said in Scripture about Christians understanding God's Word for themselves:

> These things I have written to you concerning those who try to deceive you. But the anointing which you have received from Him abides in you, and you do not need that anyone teach you; but as the same anointing teaches you concerning all things, and is true, and is not a lie, and just as it has taught you, you will abide in Him (1 John 2:26,27).

If you are a Christian, you can understand the Bible, including the prophecy passages, and especially those verses that God designed to motivate His children to live holy lifestyles. Our Lord promised, "When He, the Spirit of truth, has come, He will guide you into all truth...and He will tell you things to come."

But first, let's examine *why Christians should study prophecy.*

2

WHY CHRISTIANS SHOULD STUDY PROPHECY

God has given us three important signs that He is a supernatural God. The first is creation, the second is Jesus Christ, His Son, and the third is His written revelation of Himself that we call the Bible.

Creation provides ample evidence that He exists (Romans 1:19,20). Because it is totally impossible to get order out of disorder, only a blatant skeptic would deny that the magnificent order in this well-designed universe demands some Superdesigner. All creation testifies that there was a God of creative design behind this universe and this earth, including mankind.

Jesus Christ, the most famous and influential man who ever lived, is the evidence of both God's existence and His incredible love for mankind. For God not only sent His Son Jesus into this world to identify with mankind, but to *die* for mankind, so that men and women could have their sins forgiven and then enjoy God forever.

But the very best revelation we have is the Bible. Creation is limited in what it can tell us about God; it does not reveal His love or His forgiveness—only His almighty power. Jesus the Son is the complete revelation of God for His words and actions, and His teachings were the exact expression of God. Yet they were dependent on the written Word of God for preservation and present-day discussion. We would know very little about Christ if it were not for the Bible.

Within the Bible we have a whole body of truth that testifies to the divine authorship of Scripture, and that body of truth is *fulfilled prophecy*. Only God can foretell the future. Man tries, but in time he is shown to be a fraud. D. James Kennedy, in one of his messages, tells of reading 50 prophecies in *Enquirer* magazine that were to happen in the 1970s. By the time the 1980s came to pass, not one of them had been fulfilled!

The Bible, however, is filled with prophecies that have come to pass—prophecies about Israel, about the Gentile nations, and most important of all, about the Messiah. The fact of fulfilled prophecy is how we can know without a doubt that Jesus Christ is the Messiah of God: More than 100 prophecies of His first coming were fulfilled in His birth, life, and death!

And that is why we can be so confident that He is coming again. In fact, someone has counted eight times as many prophecies regarding Christ's *second* coming as for His *first* coming! But as comforting and exciting as that certainty is, it will be of no help to the Christian unless he studies it for himself, or it is taught to him by someone else. There are, of course, other reasons for studying this very important subject. Consider the following.

1. *God must consider prophecy important, for He has put so much of it in the Bible.*

The Bible is not a single book but is actually a library of books, of which almost one-third are prophetic writings. Of God's 66 volumes to mankind, you will find that most of the books were written by prophets. Even Moses, the lawgiver and author of the first five books of the Old Testament, was a prophet. In fact, most of God's messengers to man—including Samuel, Elijah, Daniel, and John the Baptist—were prophets. In the New Testament, there was a special first-century gift known as the "gift of prophecy." Peter, Paul, James, Jude, and others had that gift. Our Lord, of course, knew all things, and He gave the most definitive prophecy of things still to come in His Olivet Discourse. There are 16 books on prophecy in the Old Testament, including the Minor and the Major Prophets. In the New Testament, God used four books to cover the subject—Revelation, 1 and 2 Thessalonians, and Jude. In addition, many of the other books include long prophetic passages or subjects, such as our Lord's Olivet Discourse in Matthew 24 and 25. The fact that so much of Scripture is called prophecy makes it clear that God intended for His children to study it. If we omit the study of prophecy as too controversial, too difficult, or complex, we will omit almost one-third of the entire Bible!

2. Prophecy reveals our Lord as He really is.

One of the reasons I have always loved prophecy is because of the exalted view it gives of our Lord. The prophetic portrayal of Christ is different than that of the Gospels, which tell the wonderful story of His humiliation, including His birth, suffering, and death. In order to "taste death for everyone," Christ had to humble Himself and make Himself "lower than the angels" (Hebrews 2:9); and during His time on earth, He was abused by mankind. It was not a pretty sight to see our Lord abused, rejected, and crucified by His creation.

But the second coming is a different matter! Never again will Jesus Christ come into this world to suffer or be subject to the whims of man. The next time He comes it will be "in power and great glory" as "King of kings and Lord of lords." At that coming the Bible says that "every eye shall see him" (Revelation 1:7 KJV) and that "every knee [shall] bow, of those in heaven, and of those on earth, and of those under the earth, and that every tongue [shall] confess that Jesus Christ is Lord, to the glory of God the Father" (Philippians 2:10,11).

3. A proper understanding of prophecy arms the believer against cults and false prophets.

Scripture teaches that false Christs and false teachers will arise in the last days. Although there have always been false teachers, their numbers will increase as we approach the end times. The best defense is to "put on the full armor of God so that you can take your stand against the devil's schemes" (Ephesians 6:11 NIV). Our Lord predicted that these false Christs and false prophets will be able to perform great signs and miracles and deceive even the elect—that is, believers who do not know the Scriptures well, particularly those Scriptures that relate to future things.

A good illustration of this is the Jehovah's Witnesses, who came on the religious scene at the latter end of the nineteenth century. They predicted that a special group of 144,000 witnesses of Jehovah would arise just before the coming of Christ, and that they were commissioned to recruit them. Those Christians who understood Revelation 7:5-8 (from which Jehovah's Witnesses claim to get this teaching) were not deceived, for they knew that those 144,000 witnesses would arise during the coming tribulation period, and that all of the witnesses would be Jews. (The Jehovah's Witnesses are primarily Gentiles.) In 1960 the Witnesses realized that they had recruited more people into their membership than 144,000, so they changed their interpretation of prophecy to fit their growth. From then on, they began teaching that only special members who did a lot of witnessing got into the 144,000 that would go to heaven. The rest were promised that they would "in-herit the earth."

A more recent illustration is the man who sold 300,000 books explaining his claim that Christ was coming in September of 1988. The date came and went, and he realized he was wrong. So he refigured his teaching and decided he had missed the date by exactly one year—so he put out another book. This one sold only 30,000 copies! Many individuals, on the basis of this false teaching, are said to have sold their homes, quit their jobs, and begun "awaiting the Lord's return." Such Christians would have known better if they had been taught the simple fact in our Lord's prophetic discourse regarding the time of His coming: "Of that day and hour no one knows, no, not even the angels of heaven, but My Father only" (Matthew 24:36).

A good rule to follow about any teacher of prophecy who sets a day or hour for the coming of Christ is this: *Don't believe him!* As our Lord said, "Many will come in My name, saying, 'I am the Christ,' and will deceive many" (Matthew 24:5). The best way to avoid being deceived by the false teachers is to know the prophetic teachings of the Word of God.

4. *The study of prophecy promotes an evangelistic church.*

The most evangelistic periods of church history have been times when the church studied prophecy. The church at Thessalonica, an infant church to which Paul taught the truths of prophecy, was an evangelistic church. So also was the early church as a whole. From the time that our Lord said, "I will come again and receive you unto myself," the early church had an evangelistic fire that lasted almost three centuries. True, it was a persecuted church, but part of the reason it was persecuted was because of its evangelistic fire that was due in part to the prominent teaching of our Lord's soon return.

Later, when paganism was brought into the church in about the fourth century, the Bible was no longer taught widely. What's more, certain religious leaders felt the Bible shouldn't be read or handled by the common people. That was the view during the Dark Ages— an era dark toward the truths of the Word of God, for the Bible was put into museums but not read. That is why John Wycliffe (1330–1384) is considered one of the greatest Christian leaders of all time. In the fourteenth century he determined to translate the Word of God into the common language so that everyone could read it for himself. He was called "the morning star of the Reformation," and the Bible began to be studied again. In the nineteenth century came the rediscovery of the study of prophecy, or the study of last things. It was during this period that the greatest missionary and evangelistic emphasis of the modern church era was born. Throughout the past century some of the most evangelistic and missionary-minded churches were those that taught prophecy, especially the prophecies of our Lord's soon return.

The study of prophecy is also helpful in counteracting the materialism of this present age. I need not convince the reader of this book that we live in a materialistic age that is not conducive to sacrifice or spiritual dedication. Even some Christians have gotten caught up in materialistic pursuits that distract from their relationship with God. But those who study Bible prophecy recognize that this world is very temporary. One day "all these things will be burned up," and, as the Scripture asks, "Then whose shall these things be?" The Christian untaught in prophetic truth is prone to get the idea that "all things continue as they were...where is the promise of His coming?" But the promise is there; it just needs to be found in the study of prophecy.

5. *The study of prophecy tends to purify the believer.*

It is no secret that we live in an unholy age. Unfortunately, too much of that unholiness is found even in the church. One tool which the Holy Spirit uses to help believers live holy lives is the study of prophecy, particularly those passages that relate to our Lord's soon return. The apostle John said this about those who hold to the promise of the Lord's second coming: "Everyone who has this hope in Him purifies himself, just as He is pure" (1 John 3:3).

Many a believer, including this writer, has in a moment of temptation thought, "Do I want to be doing this when Christ returns?" When the answer is a resounding "NO!" it is easier to reject the temptation. Instead, we are challenged to so live that when He comes we will be found doing those things that will earn the praise, "Well done, good and faithful servant," rather than the rebuke that will be extended to those who are "ashamed before Him at His coming." It is my prayer that the study of the exciting prophecies we shall examine in this book will produce a heightened degree of holiness in your life so that you will be ready when Jesus comes.

6. *Prophecy offers confident hope in a hopeless age.*

Human beings can absorb many pressures in life, but lack of hope is not one of them. The world in which we live has no hope. Looking back, we see an unending history of war, war, war, all of which reveals the inhuman traits of mankind. The very study of history is a study of war and man's inhumanity to his fellow man. Yet the whole world yearns for peace, but knows no peace. Even the world's greatest thinkers have no workable solutions to the myriad problems facing humankind. Prophecy students, however, not only know what our loving God has planned for the future of this planet and the billions who live on it, but they have a firm confidence (that is the biblical definition of "hope") toward the future and are not afraid. We can say, "If we live, praise the Lord. If we die, praise the Lord!" Or we can say with the early Christians, "Even so, come, Lord Jesus." Those Christians had a greeting that needs to be rekindled in the church today: "Maranatha" (1 Corinthians 16:22), which means "O Lord, come." The student of prophecy will not dread the uncertain future, for he not only knows some of the things that "must come to pass," but he also knows the One who holds the future.

The sad part is that the worst days in world history are not behind us but are still ahead. Our Lord Himself warned that toward the end of human history as we have known it there would be a time of "great tribulation, such as has not been since the beginning of the world until this time, no, nor ever shall be" (Matthew 24:21). When we study that passage in detail, we see that this terrifying future will be unparalleled in human history. Yet it should offer no great personal concern for the Christian who rightly understands God's prophetic plan as it is outlined in the Scriptures, for he is confident of his place in God's plan. Unfortunately, many Christians unnecessarily experience the same distress and insecurity that unbelievers experience when they read about the things destined to come upon the earth.

This confidence (or "hope," as it is called in Scripture) is not automatic; it comes in response to the study not just of the Word of God in general but of those passages that pertain to prophecy. You may wonder why I call "hope" as it appears in Scripture "confidence." But that is what the biblical word "hope" literally means. Because of our faith in the Lord of the future, which is strengthened by our study of the Word of God, we do not look to the future with a casual understanding of hope, saying, "We hope things will turn out all right." No, we are *confident* that the future will happen exactly as Christ predicted. We do not merely wish that Jesus will come again; we are *confident* that He *will* come again, because He promised He would. The more we know about God's prophetic promises, the more convinced we will become of their future reality.

If, as many prophecy scholars believe, we begin to see world governments merge into one federated government over which one key leader will rule, Christians need not become unduly worried, for that would be just one more sign that the coming of the Lord is near. The same is true in regard to the other signs predicted for the end of the age, such as earthquakes, famines, pestilences, a spirit of lawlessness, and the disintegration of the family. Informed Christians will enjoy a "peace that passes all understanding" as a result of knowing the prophetic Word.

Ultimately, Bible prophecy predicts the destruction of Satan by the Lord Jesus Christ. Currently Satan is "the god of this age" (2 Corinthians 4:4), and that is why it seems that evil continually overcomes good. But prophecy tells us that on the day when Our Lord comes He will chain Satan in the bottomless pit, where he will "deceive the nations no more" (Revelation 20:3). And ultimately the Lord will triumph over Satan forever. Christians who know nothing about these future events will have little confidence or hope as they face the future. Only those who are familiar with prophecy can face what seems to be an uncertain future with peaceful confidence.

3

THE CERTAINTY OF CHRIST'S SECOND COMING

One of the most incredible discoveries of George Gallup's surveys of religion was that more than 62 percent of the American people believe that Jesus Christ will return literally to this earth. (The same percentage believe in the unique deity of Christ.) What makes this statistic so amazing is that the same survey indicated that 40 percent of the American people profess a born-again experience with Jesus Christ. In other words, 22 percent more Americans believe in our Lord's second coming than are ready to meet Him when He does come! That in itself should be a tremendous motivation for us to share our faith so that those 22 percent can receive Him. Taken another way, more than two out of every ten people already believe enough about Christ to receive Him personally.

The second coming of Christ, as we have already seen, is mentioned eight times more frequently in the Old and the New Testaments than His first coming. In fact, Christ's second coming is evidently the second-most-important doctrine in the entire New Testament, for the only teaching mentioned more frequently is the subject of salvation! His coming is mentioned 318 times in the New Testament alone, and that is more often than there are chapters from Matthew to Revelation (216)! What's more, all nine authors of the New Testament mentioned it.

To let you really get a feel for the extensive scriptural coverage of this subject, and to acquaint you with the unique approach this book takes in helping study prophecy for yourself, please get a pencil or pen and fill in the study guide on the next few pages after carefully examining the scriptures listed. Don't try to look for some hidden meaning in each text, but simply answer the questions or write down the obvious meanings of the verses in the space allotted.

≈ ≈ ≈

The Certainty of Christ's Second Coming

Matthew 24. Describe Christ's second coming as depicted in—

verse 27:

verse 30:

Mark 13:27. What will Christ do when He comes?

Luke 21:25-28. What do you conclude from the fact that Jesus mentioned this coming in Matthew, Mark, and Luke?

John 14:1-3. What specific promise did our Lord make here?

Acts 1:10,11. Quote the angel's promise.

Philippians 3:20,21. Where will Christ come from, and what will He do when He comes?

1 Thessalonians 3:13. How does God want us to be when Christ comes?

2 Thessalonians 2:1. What is the subject of this chapter?

James 5:8. How should we live as we await Christ's return?

Jude 14,15. List three things this passage states about the Lord's return.

≈ ≈ ≈

The preceding scriptures are only a few of the 318 references in the New Testament referring to the second coming of the Lord, but they will give you a feel for the fact that it is an extremely prominent subject in the biblical record. Christ's second coming is clearly mentioned or alluded to in 23 of the 27 New Testament books, and of the four books that make no clear mention of it, three of these

(Philemon, 2 John, and 3 John) are short, one-chapter personal letters. Only one doctrinal book makes no specific mention of the subject (Galatians), although an implied reference to the event appears
in 1:4.

To help you appreciate the New Testament's emphasis on the
coming of Christ, I would like to take you on a quick tour through
its 27 books, one at a time.

Matthew. Two entire chapters, 24 and 25, are devoted to this subject. Often called "the Olivet Discourse," this message was delivered
just prior to our Lord's death. This sermon contains the most important and complete chronology of future events found in Scripture
with the exception of the book of Revelation.

Mark. Mark devotes chapter 13 to the Olivet Discourse prophecies of the end times, culminating in the second coming of Christ.

Luke. This great first-century historian and doctor included the
second coming prophecies in chapters 17 and 21 of this book. He
wrote, "Then they will see the Son of Man coming in a cloud with
power and great glory" (21:27).

John. The "beloved disciple," who outlived all the other apostles, wrote his life of Christ about 50 years after Christ ascended
into heaven. Although he does not repeat the Olivet Discourse covered by the other three Gospel writers, he quotes one of the clearest promises to come from the Savior's lips on this subject:

> Let not your heart be troubled, you believe in
> God, believe also in Me. In My Father's house are
> many mansions; if it were not so, I would have told
> you. I go to prepare a place for you, I will come again
> and receive you to Myself, that where I am, there
> you may be also (14:1-3).

Acts. Luke's excellent record of the work of the Holy Spirit
through the lives of the apostles contains several promises of
Christ's second coming. The first act of the ascended Christ was to
dispatch two angelic messengers who announced to His disciples:
"Men of Galilee, why do you stand gazing up into heaven? This
same Jesus, who was taken up from you into heaven, will so come in
like manner as you saw Him go into heaven" (1:11).

In addition, the first sermon Peter preached after the day of Pentecost records this promise given to the Jews of Jerusalem, many of whom had doubtless participated in calling for the death of Christ: "Repent therefore and be converted, that your sins may be blotted out, so that times of refreshing may come from the presence of the Lord, and that He may send Jesus Christ, who was preached to you before" (3:19,20). The acts of the first century apostles were motivated by both the Holy Spirit and the expectation of the return of Jesus to this earth.

Thirteen Epistles of Paul. The writings of the apostle Paul had a tremendous impact on the early church. Paul imparted deep doctrinal teaching, practical exhortation, correction, and instruction on many aspects of the Christian life. Thirteen times he mentioned baptism, and only twice did he touch on communion, yet he mentioned the second coming of our Lord 50 times.

First Thessalonians is considered the first letter Paul wrote. In it he referred the young believers at Thessalonica to the second coming of Christ in every chapter! (see 1:10; 2:19; 3:13; 4:13-18; 5:2,23). He repeated that emphasis in even greater detail in 2 Thessalonians (see 1:7-10; 2:1-12; 3:5). These epistles demonstrate how early and insistently Paul taught new converts the doctrine of Christ's return, for he was in their city only three weeks before angry Jews drove him out of town.

The apostle's love of the second coming is also seen in his rather stern words at the conclusion of 1 Corinthians: "If anyone does not love the Lord Jesus Christ, let him be accursed. O Lord, come!" (16:22).

The Greek word Paul used in that last phrase, *maranatha*, means "the Lord is coming." That expression gained popularity in the first century and became a common mode of greeting and parting. Christians often included it in letters, and in some cases even soldiers used it as a slogan when they went off to war.

All but two of Paul's epistles contain one or more references to the second coming. It is obliquely cited in Romans 11:26 and in 14:10, where he talks about the judgment seat of Christ. That judgment is described in detail in 1 Corinthians 3:9-15. Then in 1 Corinthians chapter 15 Paul not only describes the resurrection of the body, but gives details of the rapture in verses 50-58. He also refers to some of these same second coming truths in 2 Corinthians 1:14 and 5:10. Galatians, which offers a deep discussion on the finished work of Christ on the cross, does not contain a clear reference to the second coming, though an allusion to the event appears in 1:4. Ephesians presents the Christian "in the heavenly places," and "the day of redemption" (1:3; 4:30) can only mean the day of deliverance through Christ's return. Philippians contains several references to the Lord's coming, the best of which is Philippians 3:20-21:

> For our citizenship is in heaven, from which we also eagerly wait for the Savior, the Lord Jesus Christ, who will transform our lowly body that it may be conformed to His glorious body, according to the working by which He is able even to subdue all things to Himself.

A thrilling promise appears in Colossians: "When Christ who is our life appears, then you will also appear with Him in glory" (3:4).

Like 1 and 2 Thessalonians, the epistles to Timothy provide many references to the second coming of Christ. And 2 Timothy 1:10 and 4:1,8 refer to "the appearing" and "His appearing."

The book of Titus contains the advice of a veteran servant of God to a young preacher on how to conduct the work of the Lord in the church. Paul challenges Titus to teach people to deny themselves "ungodliness and worldly lusts...[to] live soberly, righteously, and godly in the present world" (2:12).

When all the books of Paul are considered, we find that only two of 13 omit mention of the second coming, and one of these is Philemon, a personal letter of only one chapter. There is no question the apostle Paul was absolutely certain that his Lord and Savior was coming back to this earth again.

Hebrews. This is a magnificent presentation of Christ as the fulfillment of the Old Testament types and symbols. One of the promises of our Lord's return found in this book states: "So Christ was offered once to bear the sins of many. To those who eagerly wait for Him He will appear a second time, apart from sin, for salvation" (9:28).

James. This little book, which challenges Christians to show their faith by their works, culminates with a strong appeal relative to the coming of Christ: "Be patient. Establish your hearts, for the coming of the Lord is at hand" (5:8).

Peter. Writing a church that was undergoing the trials of persecution, the apostle Peter challenged the elders to be faithful leaders on the basis of the Lord's coming: "And when the Chief Shepherd appears, you will receive the crown of glory that does not fade away" (1 Peter 5:4). Peter's second epistle contains a lengthy prophecy concerning the rise of scoffers in the days just preceding Christ's coming. He promises that in spite of their ridicule, "the day of the Lord will come as a thief in the night" (2 Peter 3:10).

First John. The beautiful epistle that brings assurance of salvation and confidence to us also challenges us to holy living on the basis of Christ's second coming. One example is this: "Now, little children, abide in Him, that when He appears, we may have confidence and not be ashamed before Him at His coming" (2:28).

Jude. This tiny, one-chapter book contains a quotation from the patriarch Enoch, who walked in intimate fellowship with God during the chaotic days preceding the Flood and suddenly went directly to be with God. Genesis 5:24 says, "And Enoch walked with God, and he was not, for God took him." Some prophecy teachers suggest that Enoch's experience is symbolic of what will happen to Christians just before the chaotic days of the Tribulation, when the Lord will suddenly take Christians off this earth to be with Himself (see 1 Thessalonians 4:13-18 and 1 Corinthians 15:51-52). Before Enoch's "rapture" or sudden departure, he gave this inspired prophecy: "Enoch, the seventh from Adam, prophesied about these men also, saying, 'Behold, the Lord comes with ten thousands of His saints, to execute judgment on all, to convict all who are ungodly among them of all their ungodly deeds which they have committed in an ungodly way, and of all the harsh things which ungodly sinners have spoken against Him'" (Jude 14,15).

Revelation. The Bible ends with an entire book filled with prophecies about the second coming. It directs us to a study of things forecast from the first century after Christ's ascension all the way until the end of the world.

Although I've just listed many of the outstanding references to the Lord's second coming as found from Matthew to Revelation, this list is by no means exhaustive. There's much more material that

God has provided in His Word to establish the absolute certainty of His Son's coming back to this earth.

The sheer weight of evidence leads to the conclusion that if one believes the Bible, he must believe in the second coming of Christ. Not only was it a universal conviction and motivating factor in the life of the early church, but all nine authors of the New Testament Scriptures mentioned it. Since they universally accepted so literally our Lord's promise, "I will come again," can we do less?

Summary

While there are many disagreements among Christians about the *time* of our Lord's coming, there is little disagreement over the fact that He *will* return. We have seen several of His specific promises to return again and take us to be with Himself, and because the Bible says His word cannot fail, we know it will happen. In addition, the angels promised Jesus would return, as did the disciples many times. The apostle Paul is a good example: He mentioned the communion ordinance only twice in his 13 epistles and baptism only 13 times, but he mentioned the return of our Lord 50 times! It is one of the most frequently mentioned subjects in the Scripture, and a doctrinal necessity, for most Bible doctrines are so dependent upon it that they would not make much sense without it. It is the cornerstone of prophecy and, next to salvation, the most important doctrine in the Bible. Christ's second coming is the next major event of prophecy; as such, it is worthy of our detailed study.

The second coming is so much a part of Christianity that even unsaved people with only a limited knowledge of Scripture believe He will return to this earth. This may indicate a yearning on the part of many lost people who see the hopeless state of world affairs. Somehow they long to see a benevolent leader come on the world scene to offer peace, prosperity, and health to a war-weary, poverty-stricken, and disease-ridden world. Only Jesus Christ qualifies to be that leader! Amen

4

TWO SECOND
COMINGS OR ONE?

We might as well deal right at the beginning with the *time* of Christ's coming, the most controversial aspect of our Lord's second coming. Few, if any, Christian scholars do not recognize the *fact* of His coming again to this earth. The main controversy surrounds the subject of *when* He will return, and that includes whether He will come for His church (or all Christian believers) at one point in the future and then come for everyone else at a later date, or whether He will come for His church and all other believers at the same time.

It is imperative to point out here that fine Christians are to be found on almost all sides of this issue. It is also important to realize that while we can be dogmatic about such doctrines as the virgin birth, the deity of our Lord, the inerrancy of the Scriptures, the need to be born again, salvation by grace through faith, and certain other doctrines—including the fact of our Lord's second coming—this does not mean that we can be totally dogmatic about the *time* of His coming. The Bible gives many details associated with Christ's coming throughout the prophetic passages of Scripture, many of which have given rise to different interpretations in that the events involved are located at different times. Thus we should develop a sense of respect for those who hold a position that is different from our own.

31

The purpose of this book is to help you study the Bible's prophetic passages for yourself so you can come to a position that you can support from the Word of God. Then your beliefs will be based on personal Bible study rather than on the teachings of another person. That is why it is important for you to fill in the questions asked in the study guides in this book *before* you try to make up your own mind or before you read my summary. It may be that you will not accept my summary or interpretation, and that's fine. All I ask is that you be persuaded by the Scriptures themselves and not by someone else's interpretation of them. That is particularly true of the information in Figure 1 (p. 34), which conveys the idea that several second-coming passages seem to contradict each other. I say *seem* to contradict because there are no real contradictions in the Bible. Let us first examine these seeming contradictions, and then see if we can harmonize them.

≈ ≈ ≈

The Two Contrasting Phases of Christ's Second Coming

1 Thessalonians 4:17. In this text, locate where Christ will come.

Matthew 25:31,32. Does this occur in heaven or in the air or on the earth?

Revelation 19:15-19. When Christ comes as "King of kings and Lord of lords," where does He conquer the nations and judge the kings—in heaven or on earth?

Zechariah 14:4,9. Where specifically will Jesus come?

Mark 13:33-37. This passage describes one aspect of Jesus' coming. Select one word based on verse 37 to describe it.

Mark 13:26. Contrast that to this verse.

Matthew 24:30. This verse describes the reaction of the people who see Christ at His coming. What is it?

≈ ≈ ≈

Now examine Figure 1 and see if it represents your findings.

These are only some of the contrasting views of Christ's coming in Scripture that must be harmonized. While some Bible teachers believe that the rapture and second coming happen simultaneously, many others believe that there are two different parts or phases of His one coming.

For example, Christ is now in heaven, from which the angel promised He would come again to this earth. The first phase of His coming is "in the air" for believers; it will be a great blessing to all who participate in it. This is called by Bible scholars "the rapture," based on the Greek word *harpazo*, which means "to snatch away." The same word is used in Acts 8:39 and describes how the Holy

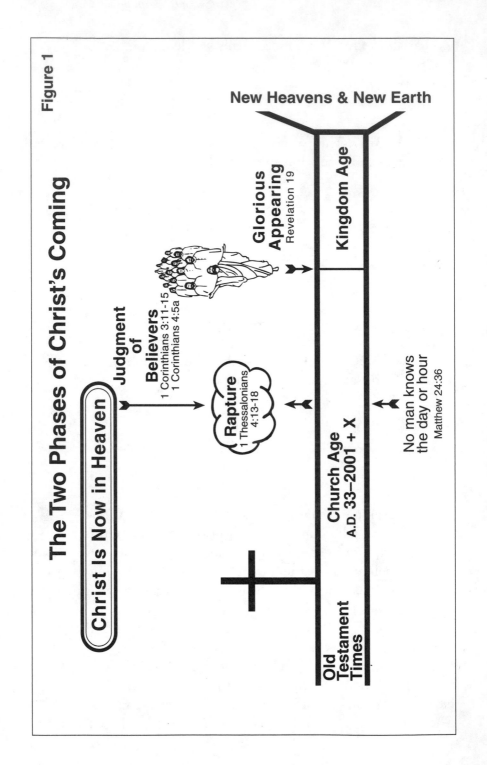

Figure 1

Spirit "caught Philip away" after he baptized the Ethiopian. Paul also used this word to describe his experience of being "caught up to the third heaven" (2 Corinthians 12:2-4). "Rapture" has come to refer to the phase of our Lord's return when He appears in the air just for Christians, who are "caught up" together with the resurrected saints who have been "asleep in Jesus."

According to 1 Thessalonians 4:13-18, which is the most complete description of the "rapture" phase of Christ's coming, the rapture is preceded by the resurrection of all Christians who have died since the founding of Christianity. They are not really dead, since their souls and spirits have been "absent from the body [at death] and [are] present with the Lord" (2 Corinthians 5:8). That is what is meant by "asleep in Jesus"—which goes on until the Lord comes. Only a few passages in the New Testament and none in the Old Testament describe the rapture phase, which will be described in detail later. But because it is a time of reuniting both dead believers and those who are "alive and remain," plus the fact that they will all "meet the Lord in the air," it is a time of great blessing called "that blessed hope" (Titus 2:13). And it is immediately after the rapture that the judgment of Christians will take place.

The second phase of the Lord's second coming is the public appearance of Christ to this earth, when He is accompanied with power and great glory as well as the angels of heaven. At that time He will set up His earthly kingdom. We call this "the glorious appearing of Christ." At that time "every eye will see Him" (Revelation 1:7), and those who rejected Him will mourn because they will finally realize who He really is and that it is now too late to accept Him by faith as Lord and Savior. The overwhelming number of references to the second coming in both the Old and New Testaments have to do with this phase of our Lord's coming; only a few references describe His coming for His church, or the rapture. *So we see that there are not two comings of Christ, but rather, there are two phases of His one coming.* The first phase is for Christians, and the second phase is for the world of unbelievers.

As you examine Figure 1 (p. 34), which is labeled "The Two Phases of Christ's Coming," you will find that the Lord leaves heaven only once—at the first phase of His coming "in the air" (the rapture), which we have seen is only for believers. Then, while still in the air, He conducts the judgment of believers. It is not well understood by Christians that all people will be judged, both believers and unbelievers. That is why we will dedicate a whole chapter to this subject. For now, however, I want you to note that the Lord remains "in the air," where He conducts this judgment of Christians and where their rewards (or lack of them) will be administered. (Believers will "rule and reign with Him" according to this judgment on the basis of what good works they performed after they became Christians.) Then, after an undisclosed period of time during which that judgment takes place, the Lord finishes His second coming by descending the rest of the way to the earth "in power and great glory, with the holy angels" to rule and reign literally during what Scripture calls the kingdom age, which we will also study in a future chapter.

What's important to observe is that this is all one coming. The two phases of Christ's one second coming are in different places, at different times, for different people, and for different purposes. Some scholars believe both phases will be fulfilled simultaneously. While this theory is held by many good people and solves some problems, it seems to this author that it creates far more problems than it solves. For one, it all but ignores the differences already pointed out. It makes no allowances for the judgment of believers—unless it is all done in an instant of time (which is possible, though not likely, since that would not allow for individual treatment and reward). In addition, this view leaves out several important events that will go on during that time.

The Rapture Phase

Now that you understand when the rapture phase of our Lord's second return occurs, let's examine those passages that deal primarily with the rapture. In the following paragraph I have reproduced the passage without comment from the New King James Version of the Bible, a highly regarded translation. These verses describe 18 steps or events in the rapture; please write them into the spaces provided for your own research.

I do not want you to be ignorant, brethren, concerning those who have fallen asleep, lest you sorrow as others who have no hope. For if we believe that Jesus died and rose again, even so God will bring with Him those who sleep in Jesus. For this we say to you by the word of the Lord, that we who are alive and remain until the coming of the Lord will by no means precede those who are asleep. For the Lord Himself will descend from heaven with a shout, with the voice of an archangel, and with the trumpet of God. And the dead in Christ will rise first. Then we who are alive and remain shall be caught up together with them in the clouds to meet the Lord in the air. And thus we shall always be with the Lord. Therefore comfort one another with these words (1 Thessalonians 4:13-18).

≈ ≈ ≈

The Rapture According to 1 Thessalonians 4:13-18

Verse 13. What kind of people did Paul *not* want the Thessalonians to be?

List Paul's two purposes for giving this teaching.

1)

2)

To whom did Paul address this teaching?

Verse 14. Whom did Paul say Jesus would bring when He comes again?

Verse 15. Where did Paul get this teaching?

What is the event Paul is describing?

Who will *not* precede dead believers?

Verse 16. List the three things that happen when the Lord descends from heaven.

1)

2)

3)

Who responds first?

Verse 17. List four things that happen in sequence.
1)

2)

3)

4)

Verse 18. Reread the last portion of verse 13 and all of verse 18, and then state why Paul wrote this passage.

≈ ≈ ≈

The Rapture According to 1 Corinthians 15:50-58

The fifteenth chapter of 1 Corinthians is the great resurrection chapter of the Bible. Only the Bible gives factual information about this event that can inspire believers. Note how closely this section of Scripture parallels the rapture passage. This passage provides more details about what will happen when the rapture occurs, and should be studied along with 1 Thessalonians 4:16,17.

Verse 50. How does Paul describe the resurrected body?

Verse 51. List two parts of this "mystery" that Paul reveals.
   1)

   2)

Verse 52. How fast will this change occur?

What does the trumpet signal?

Verses 53-57. How essential is this change into the incorruptible?

What victory does Christ give us?

Verse 58. What conclusion does Paul draw from this teaching on resurrection at the rapture?

Why?

≈ ≈ ≈

Jesus' Only Direct Reference to the Rapture

Our Lord referred directly to the rapture only once (John 14:1-3). All His other teachings on His return have to do with the second phase, or the literal, physical return when He will set up His kingdom, for which the Jews (to whom He spoke) were looking. However, the day before Jesus died on the cross He prepared His disciples to function during His absence (the church age) and addressed them with these words:

> Let not your heart be troubled; you believe in God, believe also in Me. In My Father's house are many mansions; if it were not so, I would have told you. I go to prepare a place for you. And if I go and prepare a place for you, I will come again and receive you to Myself, that where I am, there you may be also (John 14:1-3).

Describe what Jesus was saying. Specifically identify the phase of His coming that He had in mind.

Where have the disciples lived since their death until now?
14:1-2

14:3c

Note: Why do you think 1 Thessalonians 4:13-18, 1 Corinthians 15:50-58, and John 14:1-3 are the Bible passages most frequently used at the funerals of Christians?

≈ ≈ ≈

The Public, Visible Phase of Christ's Coming

We have already seen that the second phase of our Lord's coming, or the glorious appearing, is the one most frequently mentioned in the Scriptures, both in the Old and New Testaments. It is the event that all the prophets of Israel looked forward to and is the one that the disciples had in mind when they asked our Lord, "What will be *the* sign of Your coming, and of the end of the age?" (Matthew 24:3). We will study this in detail in a later chapter, but here I want to call your attention to the terms the disciples used: "the sign of your coming" and "the end of the age." When Christ comes physically to this earth, it will be to end this period of time and usher in a whole new age—not the pantheistic mysticism of the New Age movement, but a whole new age for mankind when God Himself will be the King of kings and will rule over the earth. As we shall see, this age will fulfill the fondest dreams of all those who humble themselves before God.

For a complete description of that event, read our Lord's prophecies in Matthew 24:29-31 and 25:31-46 and the apostle John's account in Revelation 19:11-21. Then read Daniel the prophet, who in the second chapter of his book, described four successive world governments. In verse 44 he predicted their successive destructions and eventual replacement by an everlasting kingdom established by God. Notice that it is "the rock cut without hands" in the king's vision that will destroy all the other kingdoms and fill the whole earth (Daniel 2:35). Christ, of course, is the "rock of ages" (see 1 Corinthians 10:4).

≈ ≈ ≈

The Glorious Appearing

Briefly summarize what the following passages teach about the glorious appearing phase of our Lord's second coming.

Matthew 24:29-31.

Matthew 25:31-46.

Revelation 19:11-21.

Daniel 2:35-44.

A Chronology of the Rapture

For your benefit, here is a detailed chronology of the rapture, along with the relevant Scripture references:

1. The Lord Himself will descend from His Father's house, where He is preparing a place for us (John 14:1-3; 1 Thessalonians 4:16).

2. He will come again to receive us to Himself (John 14:1-3).

3. He will resurrect those who have fallen asleep in Him (deceased believers whom we will not precede—1 Thessalonians 4:14,15).

4. The Lord will shout as He descends ("loud command," 1 Thessalonians 4:16 NIV). All this takes place in the "twinkling of an eye" (1 Corinthians 15:52).

5. We will hear the voice of the archangel (perhaps to lead Israel during the seven years of the Tribulation as he did in the Old Testament—1 Thessalonians 4:16).

6. We will also hear the trumpet call of God (1 Thessalonians 4:16), the last trumpet for the church. (Don't confuse this with the seventh trumpet of judgment upon the world during the Tribulation in Revelation 11:15.)

7. The dead in Christ will rise first (the corruptible ashes of their dead bodies are made incorruptible and joined together with their spirits, which Jesus brings with Him—1 Thessalonians 4:16,17).

8. Then we who are alive and remain will be changed (or made incorruptible by having our bodies made "immortal"— 1 Corinthians 15:51,53).

9. We will be caught up (raptured) together (1 Thessalonians 4:17).

10. We will be caught up in the clouds (where dead and living believers will have a monumental reunion—1 Thessalonians 4:17).

11. We will meet the Lord in the air (1 Thessalonians 4:17).

12. Christ will receive us to Himself and take us to the Father's house "that where I am, there you may be also" (John 14:3).

13. "And thus we shall always be with the Lord" (1 Thessalonians 4:17).

14. At the call of Christ for believers, He will judge all things. Christians will stand before the judgment seat of Christ (Romans 14:10; 2 Corinthians 5:10), described in detail in 1 Corinthians 3:11-15. This judgment prepares Christians for...

15. The marriage of the Lamb. Before Christ returns to earth in power and great glory, He will meet His bride, the church, and the marriage supper will take place. In the meantime, after the church is raptured, the world will suffer the unprecedented

outpouring of God's wrath, which our Lord called "the great tribulation" (Matthew 24:21).

Summary

When the 300-plus Bible references to the second coming are carefully examined, it becomes clear that there are two phases to Christ's return. These passages have far too many conflicting activities connected with His return to be merged into a single coming (15 key differences can be seen in the chart on page 47).

Since we know there are no contradictions in the Word of God, our Lord must be telling us something here. Most scholars who take the Bible literally whenever possible believe He is talking about one "coming" in two stages. First, He will come suddenly in the air to rapture His church and take believers to His Father's house, in fulfillment of His promise in John 14:1-3. There, they will appear before the judgment seat of Christ (2 Corinthians 5:8-10) and participate in the marriage supper of the Lamb (Revelation 19:1-10). Then Jesus will finish His second coming by returning to earth gloriously and publicly in great power to set up His kingdom.

THE TWO PHASES OF HIS ONE COMING

Rapture Passages

John 14:1-3	Philippians 4:5	1 Peter 1:7,13
Romans 8:19	Colossians 3:4	1 Peter 5:4
1 Corinthians 1:7,8	1 Thessalonians 1:10	1 John 2:28–3:2
1 Corinthians 15:51-53	1 Thessalonians 2:19	Jude 21
1 Corinthians 16:22	1 Thessalonians 4:13-18	Revelation 2:25
Philippians 3:20,21	1 Thessalonians 5:9,23	

Second Coming Passages

Daniel 2:44,45	Matthew 13:41	2 Peter 3:1-14
Daniel 7:9-14	Matthew 24:15-31	Jude 14,15
Daniel 12:1-3	Matthew 26:64	Revelation 1:7
Zechariah 12:10	Mark 13:14-27	Revelation 19:11–20:6
Zechariah 14:1-15	Mark 14:62	Revelation 22:7,12,20
	Luke 21:25-28	

THE 15 DIFFERENCES BETWEEN THE RAPTURE AND THE GLORIOUS APPEARING

Rapture/Blessed Hope

1. Christ comes in the air for His own
2. Rapture of all Christians
3. Christians taken to the Father's house
4. No judgment on earth
5. Church taken to heaven
6. Imminent—could happen any moment
7. No signs
8. For believers only
9. Time of joy
10. Before the "day of wrath" (Tribulation)
11. No mention of Satan
12. The judgment seat of Christ
13. Marriage of the Lamb
14. Only His own see Him
15. Tribulation begins

Glorious Appearing

1. Christ comes with His own to earth
2. No one raptured
3. Resurrected saints do not see Father's house
4. Christ judges inhabitants of earth
5. Christ sets up His kingdom on earth
6. Cannot occur for at least seven years
7. Many signs for Christ's physical coming
8. Affects all humanity
9. Time of mourning
10. Immediately after Tribulation (Matthew 24)
11. Satan bound in abyss for 1,000 years
12. No time or place for judgment seat
13. His bride descends with Him
14. Every eye will see Him
15. 1,000-year kingdom of Christ begins

5

THE TRIBULATION THAT SEPARATES THE PHASES

N ow we come to a very important part of our second-coming
studies: the events that occur between the rapture phase
and the glorious appearing phase of Christ's return. While
we have already talked about the two phases, we have not yet discussed what takes place here on the earth between the two phases.
To find out, we will have to study our Lord's very definitive Olivet
Discourse, which I have reserved for a later chapter. However, the
great Old Testament prophets, particularly Daniel, had much to say
about that time period, and the book of Revelation uses 13 chapters
to describe it in detail. This period of time is known among prophecy students as the Tribulation.

Anyone who takes the Bible literally must accept the fact that
it teaches there is a time of *tribulation* awaiting the inhabitants of
this earth (some translations refer to it as a time of "great distress").
Our Lord said of this time, "There will be great distress, unequaled
from the beginning of the world until now" (Matthew 24:21 NIV).

What's significant is that in the Bible, there is more space allo-
cated to the Tribulation than the 1,000-year kingdom, heaven, hell,
or any subject except salvation and the promise of Christ's second
coming. It is mentioned at least 49 times by the Hebrew prophets,
and at least 15 times in the New Testament, including in the following passages:

Old Testament Tribulation References

The Time of Jacob's Trouble. . . . . . . Jeremiah 30:7

The Seventieth Week of Daniel . . . Daniel 9:27

Jehovah's Strange Work. . . . . Isaiah 28:21

Jehovah's Strange Act . . . . Isaiah 28:21

The Day of Israel's Calamity . . . . . . Deuteronomy 32:35;
Obadiah 12-14

The Tribulation . . . . Deuteronomy 4:30

The Indignation . . . . Isaiah 26:20; Daniel 11:36

The Overflowing Scourge . . . . Isaiah 28:15,18

The Day of Vengeance. . . . . Isaiah 34:8; 35:4; 61:2

The Year of Recompense . . . . Isaiah 34:8

The Time of Trouble . . . . Daniel 12:1;
Zephaniah 1:15

The Day of Wrath . . . . Zephaniah 1:15

The Day of Distress . . . . Zephaniah 1:15

The Day of Wasteness . . . . Zephaniah 1:15

The Day of Desolation. . . . . Zephaniah 1:15

The Day of Darkness . . . . Zephaniah 1:15;
Amos 5:18,20; Joel 2:2

The Day of Gloominess . . . . Zephaniah 1:15; Joel 2:2

The Day of Clouds. . . . . Zephaniah 1:15; Joel 2:2

The Day of Thick Darkness . . . . Zephaniah 1:15; Joel 2:2

The Day of the Trumpet . . . . Zephaniah 1:16

The Day of Alarm . . . . Zephaniah 1:16

New Testament Tribulation References

The Day of the Lord . . . . 1 Thessalonians 5:2

The Wrath of God. . . . . Revelation 14:10,19;
15:1,7; 16:1

The Hour of Trial . . . . Revelation 3:10

The Great Day of the Wrath
of the Lamb of God . . . . Revelation 8:16,17

The Wrath to Come . . . . 1 Thessalonians 1:10

The Wrath. . . . . 1 Thessalonians 5:9;
Revelation 11:18

The Great Tribulation . . . . Matthew 24:21;
Revelation 2:22; 7:14

The Tribulation . . . . Matthew 24:29

The Hour of Judgment. . . . . Revelation 14:7

As we will see, the conditions that the Bible describes for this era have never occurred up to this time in all of world history. Thus this Tribulation period, which occupies so much space in Scripture, must be located somewhere in the future. And because of its prominence in the Bible, locating it has generated no small amount of controversy. As a general rule of thumb, the more literally a person takes the prophetic portions of Scripture, the more prone he is to believe that the Tribulation is a literal time of future trauma when the Antichrist (a real person) will rule the world. You will find a study of life on this earth during that period both interesting and traumatic. The main point of controversy is whether the church will go through this period of distress or will be raptured before it begins.

The Tribulation is generally considered to be seven years in length, based on Daniel's prophetic vision of 9:24-27. In this vision the prophet was told that "70 weeks" (or 70 *heptads*, meaning 70 times seven weeks of years, for a total of 490 years) were "determined for your people [the Jews] and for your holy city." He then

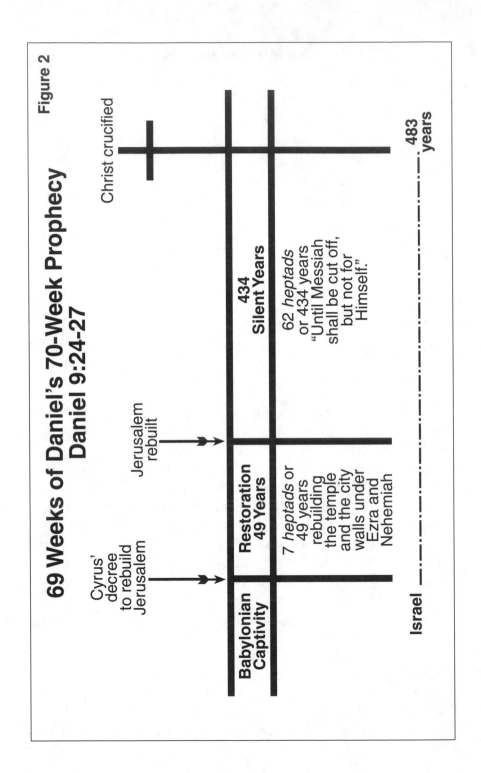

69 Weeks of Daniel's 70-Week Prophecy
Daniel 9:24-27

Figure 2

Christ crucified

Jerusalem rebuilt

Cyrus' decree to rebuild Jerusalem

Babylonian Captivity

Restoration 49 Years

7 *heptads* or 49 years rebuilding the temple and the city walls under Ezra and Nehemiah

434 Silent Years

62 *heptads* or 434 years "Until Messiah shall be cut off, but not for Himself."

Israel

483 years

lists three periods of time, beginning with seven weeks (or 49 years) "from the going forth of the command to restore and rebuild Jerusalem" (which is described in the book of Ezra and Nehemiah as the time when the walls and the temple were rebuilt). The second period was "62 weeks" (or 434 years) until "Messiah shall be cut off, but not for Himself." (This is an obvious reference to the period from the rededication of the temple to the crucifixion of Jesus the Messiah.) That leaves one *heptad* (or one seven-year period) of tribulation for the Jews that has never been fulfilled. This is usually called the "time of Jacob's trouble," which is described in Jeremiah 30:3-11. It is also described by our Lord in the Olivet Discourse and in the book of Revelation, where it is called "the tribulation." Study Figure 2 carefully.

Only 69 *heptads* (weeks of years) have been fulfilled so far. One *heptad* of seven years has never been fulfilled. The church age began immediately after the descent of the Holy Spirit on the day of Pentecost, and therefore the remaining period "determined" for Israel is yet future. Keep in mind that this prophecy of Daniel is about *Israel;* it was not given to or about the church. It was given to explain about what would happen to the Jews, and therefore no mention is made of the church. Notice instead that Daniel 9:26b points out that "the prince who is to come" (which can only be the Antichrist) will be a Roman, for it says that his people (the Romans of A.D. 70) "shall destroy the city and the sanctuary."

So in the midst of talking about the rebuilding of the temple and the holy city (during 49 years), Daniel predicted that it would be used for 434 years, then "Messiah shall be cut off." Isaiah 53 describes this "cutting off," or the crucifixion, as the details of Isaiah 53 match the descriptions of Christ's death as given in the Gospels. Then after an unspecified period of time the temple would be destroyed. Historically that took 40 years. After another undesignated period of time (the church age, which really began at Pentecost and has gone on for more than 1,900 years) there would be a period in which "there will be war; desolations are determined." A quick glance at these 1,900-plus years of church history will reveal that it has been a continuous period of wars, from the Caesars to the Saracens, from the Turks to the Mongols, from the Crusades to the wars and revolutions of the Western world.

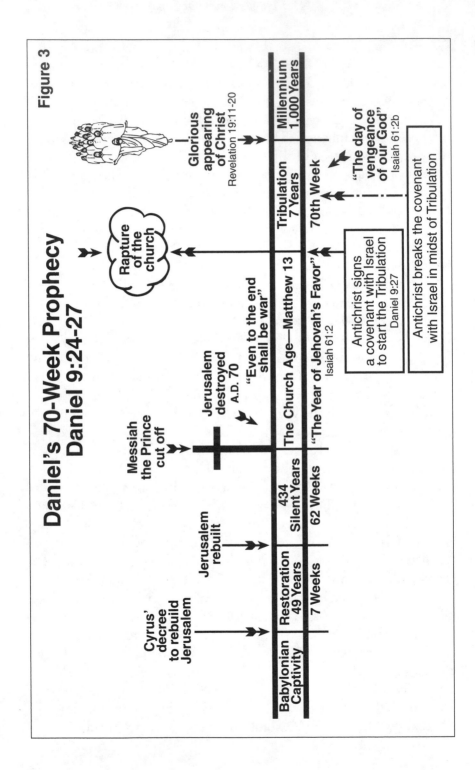

Figure 3

Daniel's 70-Week Prophecy
Daniel 9:24-27

Then Daniel 9:27 says, "He [the prince who is to come] shall confirm a covenant with many for *one week*, but in the middle of the week he shall bring an end to sacrifice and offering" (emphasis added). This is obviously a future event, and because it parallels prophetic teachings in 2 Thessalonians 2 and the book of Revelation, most prophecy teachers believe that the Antichrist will be the one who officially begins the tribulation period by signing a covenant with Israel for seven years (that unfulfilled seven years in Daniel 9). He will then break that covenant in three-and-a-half years (or 42 months, as Revelation 13 says), after which the end (the "consummation") comes: the physical return of Christ to this earth to set up His kingdom. A study of Figure 3 makes this clear.*

---

*This chart is reproduced from Tim LaHaye, *Revelation Illustrated and Made Plain* (Grand Rapids: Zondervan, 1973, 1975), p. 93.

6

THE TRIBULATION, THE
HEART OF THE BOOK OF
REVELATION

The best way to decide whether the seven-year Tribulation is yet future is to examine the events forecast to happen during that time. And the best place to analyze those events is in the book of Revelation, because more details are given there about that period than in any other place in the Bible, including our Lord's extensive references to it in Matthew 24.

Keep in mind as you read that Revelation chapters 6 and 7 go together and cover the first quarter of the Tribulation. Chapters 8 and 9 then cover the second quarter. Chapter 11 culminates at that halfway point, and chapter 13 begins there and runs simultaneously with chapter 16. While there are other subjects addressed in the book, the three sets of judgments described in chapters 6–7, 8–9, and 16 are chronological and go together with the other two chapters I have cited. These will provide you ample evidence to see for yourself if these prophecies have been fulfilled in history or are events that are yet future.

It is very important that you complete the next study guide so that you can see for yourself how simple it is to understand the book of Revelation if you let the Bible mean what it says. (For example, some of chapter 9 refers to activities in the spirit world that seem to have a physical effect on human beings.) By reading Revelation chapters 6–16 and answering the following questions as you read, you should be able to discern for yourself these important events.

~ ~ ~

The Seal Judgments of the Tribulation
Revelation 6

The first four seal judgments are the four horsemen. What effect do they have on the earth after they appear?

1) 6:1,2—

2) 6:3,4—

3) 6:5,6—

4) 6:7,8—

Describe briefly what the fifth seal reveals in 6:9-11.

Read Revelation 6:12-16 and summarize the events.

What is this period of time called (Revelation 6:17)?

~ ~ ~

The 144,000 Witnesses
Revelation 7

Revelation 7:1-17. What are these people called (verse 3b)?

Who are they (verses 4-8)?

Describe the great multitude mentioned in verses 9-14.

Note verse 14. Who are these people?

What is their reward (verses 15-17)?

The seventh seal introduces the seven trumpet judgments, which is why many prophecy students consider these judgments to be chronological: The first six seals cover 21 months, then the breaking of the seventh seal introduces the next seven trumpet judgments, which take place during the second quarter or the second 21 months of the first half of the Tribulation. The sealing of the 144,000 "servants of our God" probably occurs at the beginning of this period, and they witness all during it, along with the special two witnesses described in Revelation chapter 11. Then next, we have the trumpet judgments.

≈ ≈ ≈

The Trumpet Judgments
Revelation 8 and 9

Describe the events that take place on earth when the first trumpet sounds (8:6,7).

The second (verses 8,9).

The third (verses 10,11).

The fourth (verse 12).

The fifth (9:1-11).

The sixth (verses 12-19).

Note how the majority of people respond to these events (verse 20a).

List the six major sins of people during those days (verses 20,21).

1)

2)

3)

4)

5)

6)

≈ ≈ ≈

The Two Witnesses

In the last days, God will have the gospel message proclaimed worldwide so that people are without excuse about making a decision for Christ. During the first half of the Tribulation God not only uses the 144,000 Israelites from each of the 12 tribes who reach "a multitude which no one could number" (Revelation 7:9), but He also establishes in and around Jerusalem two special witnesses endowed with supernatural powers (Revelation 11:3-6).

During the Tribulation, two powerful opposing forces will be at work at the same time: 1) the 144,000 servants of God will bring forth a mighty soul harvest, and 2) the enormous sinfulness of those who refuse to repent. It will be the same as in our day right now, with the church witnessing for her Lord on the one hand, and those who reject the Savior on the other, except that the opposing forces will be intensified during the tribulation period.

Also, because the civil government described in Revelation 13 will be under the total control of the Antichrist and his evil forces, Christians will be persecuted and martyred in large numbers. Many people will become saved through the soul harvest, but for a while, it will seem as if Christians are on the losing end of the battle because the Antichrist is in control of the world. However, we know that ultimately, Christ—and His people—will be the victor.

≈ ≈ ≈

God's Two Supernatural Witnesses
Revelation 11

What important structure will be in place (which is not standing now—11:1)?

Who will control the city of Jerusalem at that time?

Describe the two witnesses.

How long will their ministry last (verse 3)?

Describe what happens to the two witnesses after they finish their ministry (verse 7-10).

How do the evil people who dislike the witnesses express their hatred (verses 9,10)?

What means of communication is necessary to fulfill verse 9? Could that have been possible before the present generation?

Then what happens to the two witnesses?

Many Christians believe that these two witnesses are Old Testament characters because the things they will do are so similar to what the Old Testament personages did when they were on the earth. What two Old Testament men do they remind you of?

≈ ≈ ≈

The Antichrist

Whenever the Bible uses the term "beast" symbolically (as in the description of a beast with seven heads, ten horns, and a mouth speaking blasphemy), it's referring to a *government*. An example is found in Daniel chapters 7 and 8. Most governments are repressive and persecute the common people; they usually hate God and try to keep people from worshiping Him. The Caesars and the past Communist dictators are obvious examples of this. The "beast" pictured in Revelation 13 is obviously the head of the coming world government because he so definitely takes on the functions of a person. In fact, he is joined in this chapter by a "false prophet" who is also human. We will study the Antichrist later in other Bible passages, but it is important to know from Revelation 13 some of what he will do when he assumes power. We know that he will be in power during all seven years of the Tribulation, but Revelation 13 deals primarily with the last half, when the Antichrist will have almost total control of the people living on the earth, which is why our Lord referred to that time period as the "great tribulation" (Matthew 24:21).

≈ ≈ ≈

The Beast of Revelation 13

Read the entire chapter.
The "dragon" in Scripture refers to the devil. What three things will he give the beast in verse 2?

1)

2)

3)

What kind of following will he have (verse 3c)?

Who will be their object of worship?

How will he use his mouth (verses 5,6)?

How long will he have this total control (verse 5b)?

Name the three objects of his blasphemy (verse 6).

What does verse 7a suggest to you?

Does it seem that the worldwide evangelism of the first 42 months will continue at the same pace in the second 42 months?

Then what will happen (verses 7,8)?

Who are the only ones who do not worship the beast (verse 8)?

Who are these people? To answer that question, you should also read Philippians 4:3 and Revelation 3:5.

What is God's challenge to the saints living during these days?

In summarizing the events described in verses 1-10, who is the Antichrist's (beast's) war against, and who will suffer?

≈ ≈ ≈

The False Prophet of Revelation 13

Whenever a political leader tries to exterminate religion or the true worship of God, he often begins by using the services of a false religious leader. The Antichrist will be no different. His leader will look "like a lamb" and speak "like a dragon" (verse 11). What does that suggest to you?

Where will this leader get his power (verse 12)?

What will he do with it?

What other powers will he have (verse 13)?

What effect will that have (verse 14a)?

Describe the image (verses 14b-15).

Describe the mark of the beast (verses 16,17).

What effect will the mark have on the economy?

Six is the biblical number of man. What significance do you attach to the number in verse 18?

Summarize what life will be like for both the saved and unsaved who are living on the earth at this time, as described in Revelation 13.

If you take these events to be literal happenings, is there any possible way they could refer to anything that has already occurred in world history?

Note: More details of the last 42 months of the Tribulation are described in Revelation 16. Keep in mind that the events wrought by the bowl judgments will occur during the time that the Antichrist rules the world, with the false prophet as his religious leader.

~ ~ ~

The Bowl Judgments of Revelation 16

Each of the bowls, when poured out, introduces another judgment upon the earth. In the spaces below, describe what happens on earth, and note the reaction of mankind.

First bowl (verse 2):

Reaction:

Second bowl (verse 3):

Reaction:

Third bowl (verse 4):

Reaction:

Fourth bowl (verses 8,9):

Reaction:

Fifth bowl (verses 10,11):

Reaction:

Sixth bowl (verses 12-16):

Reaction:

What famous future war is mentioned here (verses 14c,16c)?

Verse 15 is parenthetical. Could this indicate that even at this late date in the tribulation period there will still be Christians on the earth?

Seventh bowl (verses 17-21):

Reaction:

This greatest-ever earthquake will occur at the same time as the events in Revelation 18, when God will destroy Babylon, the governmental and financial capital of the world. The events of chapter 17 will occur in the middle of the Tribulation, when the kings of the earth destroy the religions of the world so that the worship of Antichrist can become the world religion.

The seventh bowl judgment concludes the Tribulation period, and Revelation 19 reveals the next chronological event, which is the physical return of Christ to this earth, or "the second coming." When He comes, He will dispose of the Antichrist and the false prophet.

How will Christ deal with the Antichrist and false prophet (19:20)?

God's justification for what He will do to those who reject Him is given in Revelation 16:5-7. What does this passage teach that the godless will do during this period?

On the chart below, based on what you have studied so far, draw your own time line describing the Tribulation. Do this before you look at Figure 4 (shown later in this chapter).

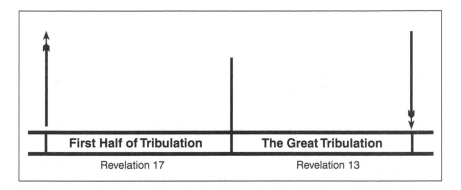

First Half of Tribulation	The Great Tribulation
Revelation 17	Revelation 13

≈ ≈ ≈

Three Important Questions

As you consider the events that are to take place during the Tribulation, ask yourself the important question again: Has such a series of events ever yet occurred in a seven-year period of history? The answer is a resounding *no!* In fact, none of these events have occurred even *singly* during the entire 1,900-year history of the church, nor have two men like the Antichrist and the false prophet ever inhabited and ruled over the earth. The reason this fact is important is that it will help you locate the sequence of the rapture and the physical coming of Christ to the earth. (More on this in a later chapter.)

However, there is still one extremely important question that you should ask yourself here. You probably noticed that there are only two kinds of people on the earth during the Tribulation: those who accept Christ by faith in His blood shed on the cross for their sins, and those who reject Him and instead follow the Antichrist (and who end up killing those who believe and blaspheme the name of God). These are the same two kinds of people we have today: those who have accepted Jesus by faith, and those who have not. My question is, Where do you stand? As we close this chapter, it would be good for you to answer the following two questions.

Have you ever personally invited Christ to come into your life to forgive your sin and save your soul?

If so, when?

If you haven't done so or are not sure you have, may I suggest that you do so right now? To have your name written in the Lamb's book of life, you must be one of His. And you either belong to Him, or to the world. Now, you may say, "I'm in between. I haven't accepted Him, but I don't want to follow the Antichrist either." But there is really no middle ground. Our Lord said, "He who is not with Me is against Me" (Matthew 12:30). And after what we have studied, I'm sure you don't want to be against Him. So right now, if you haven't done so yet, you can call on the name of the Lord by faith and be saved. A simple prayer of faith often goes something like this: "Dear Lord, I have sinned against You and Your law. I believe that Your Son, Jesus, died for my sin on the cross and rose on the third day from the grave. Please come into my life and forgive my sin. I give myself and my future to You." If you have not prayed a simple yet sincere prayer like this, please do so and enter your name and today's date in the space below.

Name_____ Date_____

Then tell someone about your decision, and read what Romans 10:9,10 says about becoming saved in Christ.

What Begins the Tribulation Period?

The prophecy of Daniel 9:27 tells us exactly what will start the Tribulation: when "he [the prince who is to come] shall confirm a covenant with many for one week." It seems that the Antichrist will make a covenant with the nation of Israel for seven years. This may relate to the rider on the white horse of Revelation 6, who comes in peace, for he has no arrows or implements of war in his hand. It appears that the Antichrist will offer peace to the world and make a covenant with Israel, bringing peace to the Jewish people, who will then be able to rebuild their temple and reinstate their sacrifices again—for three-and-a-half years! But "in the middle of the week [of years, or after three-and-a-half years has elapsed] he shall bring an end to sacrifice and offering. And on the wing of abominations shall be one who makes desolate" (Daniel 9:27). The Antichrist will break his covenant with the Jews in the middle of the Tribulation (which agrees with Revelation 11 and 13) and will launch the greatest time of desolation in the history of the world. How long will it last? "Until the consummation, which is determined." This is the same as "the time of the end," meaning the end of the 70 weeks or 490 years, which is the same as the "consummation" of God's dealing with the Jews and the literal coming of Christ to set up His kingdom.

In summary, then, the Tribulation will begin when the covenant of peace between the coming new world government (headed by the Antichrist) and the nation of Israel. But halfway through the seven years, the Antichrist will break that covenant and begin to persecute the nation of Israel, and they will become "desolate."

Many Christians think that the rapture of the church begins the Tribulation, but while it's possible the rapture and the signing of the covenant may take place very close together, the Bible is not specific on that subject. I have read suggestions that the two events may occur anywhere from 50 years apart to the same day. (More on this in a later chapter.)

The point here is that there has never been an Antichrist-type world ruler who has made a covenant of peace for seven years, and then broken that covenant with Israel at the halfway point. This obviously means that these events are still yet future.

Summary

If you take the descriptions in the book of Revelation literally, you are forced to come to the conclusion that no such period of tribulation has ever before occurred in history. True, this world has known problems, trials, famines, earthquakes, and pestilences, but never have events like *these* occurred—events of this magnitude. There are countries of the world where Christians have been martyred in large numbers. In fact, many Christians living during the fifteenth and sixteenth centuries, as well as those living in Communist countries during the twentieth century, thought they were in the biblical Tribulation. But even though they were in severe tribulation in a general sense, they were not in "the great tribulation." At no time in world history have we seen all the events described in Revelation come about.

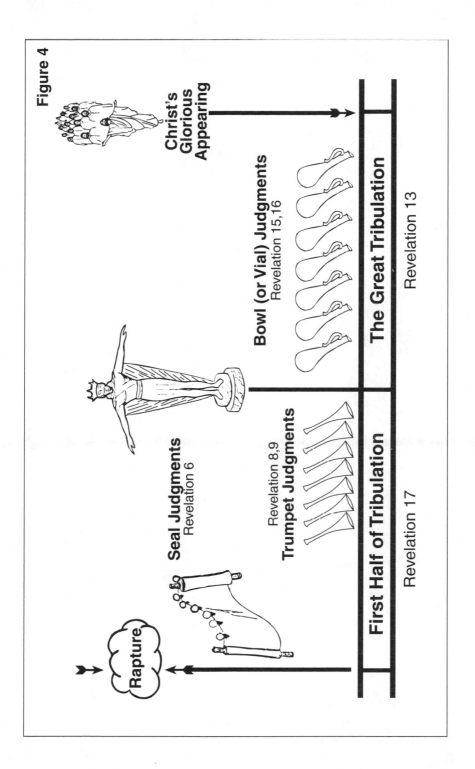

Figure 4

Rapture

Seal Judgments
Revelation 6

Revelation 8,9
Trumpet Judgments

Bowl (or Vial) Judgments
Revelation 15,16

Christ's Glorious Appearing

First Half of Tribulation
Revelation 17

The Great Tribulation
Revelation 13

7

THE RAPTURE
BEFORE THE TRIBULATION?

W ill the rapture of the church occur before the Tribulation
period begins? This is a question that has generated more
than its share of heat and not enough light from the
Scriptures. Many Christians differ on this subject, which indicates
that while Scripture is very clear on the *fact* that Christ will come
again, it is not as clear on whether He will come for His church
before, in the middle of, or at the end of the Tribulation.

There are various scriptures that are used by Christians to support the three major views. You should know your own view and be
prepared to defend it, but you should not be dogmatic to the point
of breaking fellowship with anyone who does not agree with you.
Figure 5 and the following brief synopses of each view should be
studied carefully.

The *pretribulation view* teaches that Christ will come in the air,
resurrect the dead in Christ of the church age (1 Thessalonians
4:16,17 and 1 Corinthians 15:50-56), and rapture His church up to
be with Him before the Tribulation begins, thus saving believers
from "the hour of trial which shall come upon the whole earth"
(Revelation 3:10). The world will then go through seven years of
tribulation, and then Christ will finish His coming by descending in
power and great glory to the earth to set up His millennial kingdom.

The *midtribulation view* teaches that the church will go through
the first half of the Tribulation period, and that Christ will come in

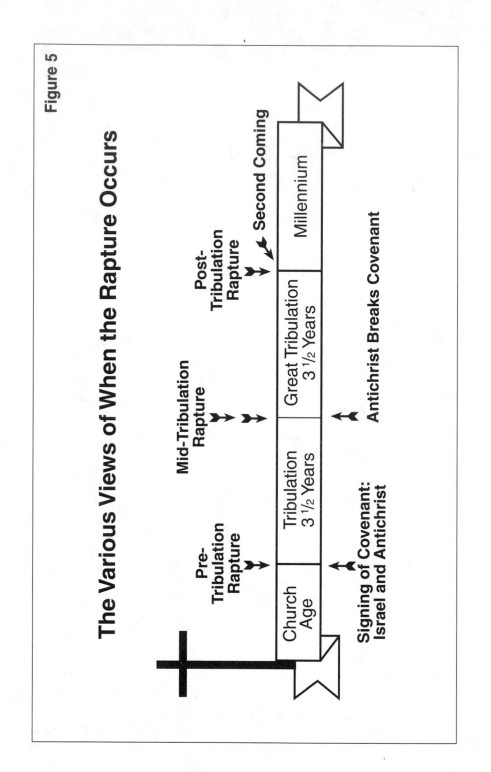

Figure 5

The Various Views of When the Rapture Occurs

Pre-Tribulation Rapture

Mid-Tribulation Rapture

Post-Tribulation Rapture

Second Coming

Church Age

Tribulation 3 1/2 Years

Great Tribulation 3 1/2 Years

Millennium

Signing of Covenant: Israel and Antichrist

Antichrist Breaks Covenant

the air to rapture His church and resurrect the dead in Christ (1 Thessalonians 4:16,17 and 1 Corinthians 15:50-56) in the middle of the seven years, prior to the great Tribulation, or the second three-and-a-half years. Then Christ will come in glory to set up His kingdom.

The *posttribulation view* teaches that the church will go through the entire Tribulation, that many church saints will be martyred, and that the Lord will resurrect dead believers up to that point and rapture those who are alive at the time by catching them up to Him as He descends, and then finish His coming to the earth in power to set up His kingdom.

You will note several similarities between these views: the resurrection of the dead, the catching up or rapture of those alive at the time, and the literal coming of Christ to the earth. Even some posttribulationists believe there will be a brief time lapse between the rapture and the glorious appearing or second coming of Christ to the earth. The main difference in these views is the timing: *When will Christ resurrect the dead saints and rapture His church?*

The three views we've just discussed represent the prevailing views of most Christians who believe that Christ will come prior to the millennial kingdom. It is good to keep in mind that sometimes a difference of opinion is determined by whether you take the prophecies about the Tribulation literally or metaphorically. Since similar tragic events have already happened before in the Old Testament (either in the plagues of Egypt or the judgments of God on Israel and the pagan nations), there is no real reason to reject the idea that the prophesied events should be taken literally and will happen exactly as predicted.

While the proponents of the midtribulation and posttribulation views may appear to have persuasive arguments, I believe that when the Bible is properly understood, we find that it teaches the rapture will occur before the Tribulation. Here are some reasons why:

1. The Lord Himself promised to deliver us.

A clear promise guaranteeing the church's rapture before the Tribulation is found in Revelation 3:10: "Since you have kept my command to endure patiently, *I will also keep you from the hour of trial that is going to come upon the whole world* to test those who live on the earth" (NIV, emphasis added). Though this promise appears in a letter written to the church at Philadelphia, we can be certain it refers to members of the universal church throughout the ages: 1) the passage refers to a future event; 2) the church of Philadelphia has long since been destroyed and disbanded; 3) this was a letter to all the churches; and 4) this promise will not be fulfilled until a time of trial that comes upon the whole world—not just the church at Philadelphia.

In addition, the word "from" (Greek, *ek*) in Revelation 3:10 literally means "out of," which is how it's rendered many other times in the Bible. God is saying, "I will keep you out of the wrath to come."

2. Only the pre-Trib view preserves imminency.

Imminency is the word used to refer to the doctrine that Christ could come at any moment to call His bride to be with Him in His Father's house. That is why Scripture has so many admonitions to watch, be ready, and to look for Him to come at any moment. The other three views destroy that immediate, at-any-time coming. In fact, those views have Christians looking not for *Christ* to come at any time, but rather for the Antichrist and the Tribulation.

3. The church is to be delivered from the wrath to come.

The promise in 1 Thessalonians 1:10 ("Jesus...delivers us from the wrath to come") was given by the Holy Spirit through the apostle Paul to a young church planted on his second missionary journey. He had only three weeks to ground this church in the Word of God before being driven out of town. Many of his teachings during that brief period evidently pertained to Bible prophecy and end-time events, for this letter—one of the first books of the New Testament to be written—emphasizes the second coming, the imminent return of Christ, the rapture, the Tribulation, and other end-time subjects. Paul apparently considered these topics essential for new converts.

Paul mentions the second coming in every chapter, so there is no doubt about the main subject of his letter. After complimenting his readers on their faith and testimony, he commends them for turning "to God from idols to serve a living and true God, and to wait for His Son from heaven, whom He raised from the dead, that is *Jesus, who rescues us from the wrath to come*" (1 Thessalonians 1:9,10 KJV, emphasis added).

The context of that passage is the rapture, for Christians are not waiting for the glorious appearing. Paul tells these people in 2 Thessalonians 2:1-12 that the latter will not occur until Antichrist (or "that lawless one") is revealed (verse 8). No, the Christians in Thessalonica were awaiting the coming of Christ for His church—that is, the rapture. They already knew the Tribulation (or "wrath to come") would follow the rapture, and that God had promised to rescue them from the wrath to come.

4. *Christians are not appointed to wrath.*

According to 1 Thessalonians 5:9, "God hath not appointed us to wrath, but to obtain salvation by our Lord Jesus Christ" (KJV). This passage, which follows the strongest passage on the rapture in the Bible (in 1 Thessalonians 4) must be considered in the light of its context.

After teaching about the rapture, Paul takes his readers to "times and...seasons" (KJV) of "the day of the Lord" (1 Thessalonians 5:1,2). Some suggest this refers to the single day on which Christ returns to this earth to set up His kingdom, but that is not consistent with the Bible's other uses of the phrase "the day of the Lord." Sometimes this phrase does refer to the glorious appearing, but on other occasions it encompasses the rapture, the Tribulation, and the glorious appearing.

For our purposes here, 1 Thessalonians 5:9 (KJV) makes it clear that God has not "appointed us to wrath" (the Tribulation) but to "obtain salvation," or deliverance from it. Since so many saints will be martyred during the Tribulation, there will be few (if any) alive at the glorious appearing of Christ. This promise cannot mean, then, that He will deliver believers *during* the time of wrath, for the saints who live through the Tribulation will *not* be delivered; in fact, most will be martyred. To be delivered out of it, the church will have to be raptured before it begins.

Since the Tribulation is *especially* the time of God's wrath, and since Christians are not appointed to wrath, then it follows that the church will be raptured *before* the Tribulation. In short, the rapture occurs before the Tribulation, while the glorious appearing occurs after it.

5. The church is absent in Revelation 4–18.

The church is mentioned 17 times in the first three chapters of Revelation, but after John (a member of the church) is called up to heaven at the beginning of chapter 4, he looks down on the events of the Tribulation, and the church is not mentioned or seen again until chapter 19, when she returns to the earth with her Bridegroom at His glorious appearing. Why? The answer is obvious: *She isn't in the Tribulation.* She is raptured to be with her Lord before it begins!

There are many other reasons for believing that the rapture occurs prior to the Tribulation; these are found in the *Tim LaHaye Prophecy Study Bible* (Chattanooga, TN: AMG Publishers, 2000), pp. 1479-82.

The pre-Trib position does not have answers for all the questions regarding the Lord's coming for His church. Since there is no one verse or passage that gives all the details of the Lord's coming in a neat little package, it is necessary to consider all the second-coming scriptures together. My conviction is that the pre-Trib rapture fits the biblical model better than any of the other views. It fits well with all that the Bible teaches about the end times, and it is a commonsense view that brings comfort to the hearts of believers, which is one of the main purposes for teaching end-times prophecy (1 Thessalonians 4:18).

8

THE CHURCH IS
DISTINCT FROM ISRAEL

Before we go any further, we should recognize that the church is not Israel, and Israel is not the church. Some of the greatest confusion today in the study of Bible prophecy is caused by teachers who say that the church has replaced Israel in God's prophetic plan. They say that there is no distinction between Israel and the church, and that the church today is spiritual Israel and that the promises God originally gave to that chosen nation now belong to the church.

But the church has not replaced Israel. The people of Israel still have a part in God's future plans. Scripture clearly indicates that the church and Israel are two separate entities. Those who say that the church is spiritual Israel have to allegorize the Bible in order to come to that conclusion. In other words, they do not interpret the prophetic passages of Scripture literally.

For a clear understanding of the church and Israel as separate entities, please complete this Bible study of Ephesians 3:1-12. As you read this passage, realize that when the New Testament talks about a "mystery," it is not referring to some mysterious teaching that cannot be understood; rather, it is talking about something that was not known in Old Testament times but is revealed to us in the New Testament.

≈ ≈ ≈

The Mystery of the Church Revealed
Ephesians 3:1-12

What was given to Paul in Ephesians 3:2?

How did he learn this "mystery"?

What does that suggest to you?

Is it possible to understand this "mystery"?

How?

Why didn't Israel, in the Old Testament, understand this (verse 5)?

How is it made known today (verse 5)?

What then is one of the purposes of the church age (verse 6)?

Would you say that the church, meaning the whole body of Christ made up of believers of all the ages, is made up primarily of Jews or of Gentiles?

Now do you see why the church is often referred to as the period of time when God works primarily with Gentiles?

What is the church's commission (verse 10)?

What does verse 11 mean?

What is the result (verse 12)?

In the days when God was working with Israel, did the Jews have this same access?

(Note: The reason they didn't have this same access is because Christ had not yet died for the sins of the world.)

≈ ≈ ≈

Israel Is Not the Church

God worked primarily through Israel in the Old Testament, and God revealed to Daniel the prophet that 490 years would "be determined" until Messiah was cut off. Then an undetermined period of time would transpire, which Isaiah called "the year of the Lord's favor" (Isaiah 61:2 NIV). Our Lord, just before He died on the cross for the sins of the whole world, began His church, which would be His primary lighthouse for proclaiming the gospel during that period of time we call "the church age," which has been going on now for over 1,900 years. However, during the end times that God told Daniel about in Daniel 12:1 (and also other prophets), God said He would fulfill the many prophecies to Israel that have not yet been fulfilled, culminating in the second coming of Messiah to set up His kingdom. Before that event, however, the unfulfilled seventieth "week" of Daniel (that is, seven years) would be fulfilled. That is what Jesus addressed in His Olivet Discourse, which we shall study later. These distinct periods of time are identified in Figure 6.

It is important to understand that God has now (since the finished work of Christ on the cross) changed His dealings with man. We are no longer under the Old Testament economy that required the blood sacrifice of animals. Christ's death, which was the final and perfect sacrifice, ushered in the new economy of God's grace to man (an economy that the book of Hebrews tells us repeatedly is "far better").

This monumental event of Messiah being "cut off, but not for Himself" (which is the crucifixion), introduced a whole new age or period of time: "the acceptable year [period of time] of the LORD's favor." We are living in that age right now—the church age. And then shall come the last portion of Isaiah's prophecy, "the day of vengeance of our God" (Isaiah 61:2 NIV), or the Tribulation, otherwise known as the seventieth week of Daniel. In this time, Israel will be at center stage once again, for the church will have been raptured.

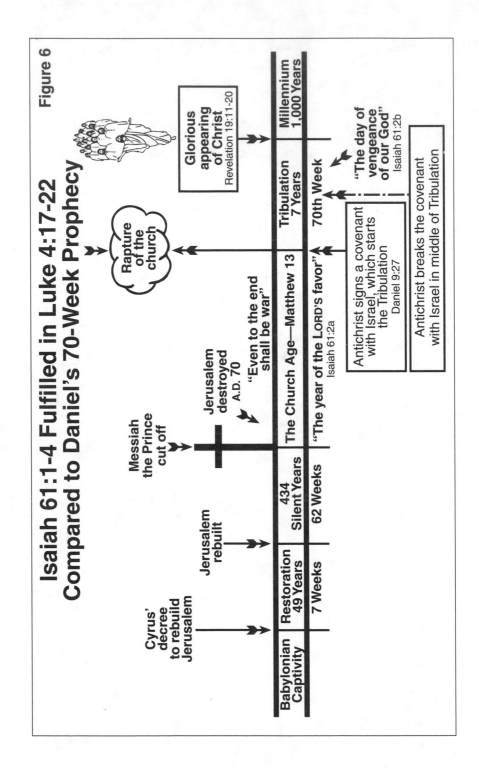

Figure 6

Isaiah 61:1-4 Fulfilled in Luke 4:17-22 Compared to Daniel's 70-Week Prophecy

Cyrus' decree to rebuild Jerusalem

Jerusalem rebuilt

Messiah the Prince cut off

Jerusalem destroyed A.D. 70

"Even to the end shall be war" Matthew 13

Rapture of the church

Glorious appearing of Christ Revelation 19:11-20

Antichrist signs a covenant with Israel, which starts the Tribulation Daniel 9:27

Antichrist breaks the covenant with Israel in middle of Tribulation

"The day of vengeance of our God" Isaiah 61:2b

| Babylonian Captivity | Restoration 49 Years | 434 Silent Years | The Church Age—Matthew 13 | Tribulation 7 Years | Millennium 1,000 Years |
| | 7 Weeks | 62 Weeks | "The year of the LORD's favor" Isaiah 61:2a | 70th Week | |

9

CHRISTIANS WILL BE SAVED
FROM THE WRATH

Not only does "the year of the Lord's favor" (NIV), or the church age, come to a distinct end, to be followed by the "day of God's wrath" (the unfulfilled period of seven years), but God has given His church ample evidence in Scripture that it will not go through the Tribulation. The reason is not that Christians deserve to be spared from it, since we don't deserve any of the blessings that God has bestowed upon us. The true reason is that *the Tribulation period is not for the church.* Instead, it is for Israel to fulfill prophecy, and for the Gentiles to be judged if they refuse to repent. Anyone who fails to distinguish between the church, Israel, and the Gentile world will have a difficult time understanding most of prophecy. Paul clearly identifies these three major people groups as distinct entities in 1 Corinthians 10:32, where he writes, "Give no offense, either to the Jews or to the Greeks or to the church of God."

The church is really made up of both Jews and Gentiles ("Greeks") who have spiritually experienced the "born-again" relationship with Him by faith. They have entered into God's kingdom spiritually by faith, awaiting the day when they will enter His physical kingdom at Christ's second coming. Those who are in the church are not appointed to wrath (or the period of wrath), which is really for unbelieving Jews and Gentiles.

Our Lord, in His Olivet Discourse, alluded to the Christians' escape from the coming day of wrath that shall try the whole earth: "Watch therefore, and pray always that you may be counted worthy to escape all these things that will come to pass, and to stand before the Son of Man" (Luke 21:36).

In 1 Thessalonians 5:9, after talking about "the times and seasons" (5:1) and "the day of the Lord" (5:2), Paul said, "For God did not appoint us to wrath, but to obtain salvation through our Lord Jesus Christ." This is an obvious reference to the day of wrath that we saw so vividly described in Revelation 6:17, which says, "The great day of His wrath has come, and who is able to stand?" This confirms the fact that the church is not appointed to wrath but to salvation or deliverance. (Some prophecy teachers associate this wrath with the final judgment and hell, which Christians are of course exempt from also. But the context of this wrath is not hell, but the Tribulation period.)

We see this affirmed in 1 Thessalonians 1:10, where we find that Christ at His coming will deliver us "from the wrath to come." This is similar to the challenge that the Spirit of God gave to the church of Philadelphia (which many Bible teachers think represents the Bible-believing church of our own day): "Because you have kept My command to persevere, I also will keep you from the hour of trial which shall come upon the whole world, to test those who dwell on the earth" (Revelation 3:10). Notice that our Lord promised those believers they would be "kept *from the hour of trial* which shall come upon all the world" (emphasis added), and not merely kept while they go through it.

Some Bible teachers (among whom are some of my personal friends) think it weakens the church to teach that we are such Pollyanna Christians that we have to be saved from the Tribulation wrath, and that if we are wrong in our pretribulation view, this will create tragic disillusionment among believers when they find themselves going through the Tribulation. Frankly, I have more confidence in Christians than that. If we are wrong about this interpretation and wake up in the first or second half of the tribulation, I am confident that with God's help we will be able to persevere through the Tribulation.

But here is something important to consider: According to Scripture, the rapture phase of Christ's coming for His church will be *sudden and unexpected*. Except for those who "look for Him" and are "ready at His coming" (in other words, are spiritually prepared for Him), Christ's coming will catch people unprepared—after all, we do not know the hour of His coming (Matthew 24:44), and Christ will come "as a thief in the night" (1 Thessalonians 5:2). If the Lord is to come for His church *after* the Tribulation, then His coming cannot be unexpected "as a thief in the night."

If we who are Christians had to go through the Tribulation before Christ comes, then the timing of Christ's coming would no longer be a surprise. If the posttribulationist view is right, Christ will come exactly seven years from the time the Antichrist signs the covenant with Israel, or as Revelation 13 states it, two periods of 42 months. What would be surprising about that?

What's more, for believers to go through the Tribulation before Christ comes to receive them to Himself is hardly "the blessed hope" that Paul challenges Christians to look forward to. Can you imagine challenging Christians to look forward to the coming of Christ and then adding, "Oh, by the way, before He comes you must suffer the horrors of the tribulation period"!

There is another passage that contains a specific reference to Christians being removed from the world before the Tribulation comes, and that passage is 2 Thessalonians 2:3. I have not used it until now because the old King James rendering of this verse has created much unnecessary confusion: "Let no man deceive you by any means: for that day shall not come except there come *a falling away first*, and that man of sin be revealed, the son of perdition" (emphasis added). Many people have been led to believe a mid- or posttribulationist position for the rapture because of this text (since it seems to teach that Christians will "fall away" during the Tribulation). John Walvoord, in his classic book *The Rapture Question*, quotes another prophecy teacher about this verse:

> It is normally considered a reference to doctrinal apostasy. English pointed out that the word is derived from the verb *aphistemi*, used fifteen times in the New Testament, with only three of the references relating

to religious departure. In eleven of the instances, the word *depart* is a good translation. As English indicated in a note, a number of ancient versions, such as Tyndale's, the Coverdale Bible, the version by Cranmer, the Geneva Bible, and Beza's translation, all from the sixteenth century, render the term "departing." He therefore suggested the possibility of rendering 2 Thessalonians 2:3 to the effect that the departure must "come first," i.e., the rapture of the church must occur before the man of sin is revealed. If this translation be admitted, it would constitute an explicit statement that the rapture of the church occurs before the Tribulation.*

The deliverance of Christians from the world's greatest period of wrath is a gift of God for His church. It is not something she deserves, but something the Lord gives because He loves His church. In Ephesians Paul uses the symbol of a bride and groom to illustrate the relationship of Christ and His church, which is called "the bride of Christ." It seems appropriate that the perfect Groom would manifest His love by rapturing His church before the period of wrath just because He loves her. Scripture and the love of Christ, then, seems to favor the pretribulationist view of the rapture.

---

* John F. Walvoord, *The Rapture Question* (Grand Rapids: Zondervan Publishing House, 1970), pp.67-68.

10

NOT REALLY SO OBSCURE

One of the criticisms directed at the pretribulation rapture view is that the rapture is not clearly mentioned very many times in Scripture (the main passages are John 14:1-3; 1 Thessalonians 4:13-18; 1 Corinthians 15:50-56; 2 Thessalonians 2:1-12; and possibly Revelation 4:1,2.)

In addition, while we are told five times in Scripture that we are kept from the day of wrath, scores of other Scriptures refer to the final physical coming of Christ. But my question is this: How many times does the Bible have to teach something for it to be accepted as fact? You may be surprised to learn that the term "born again" occurs only three times in Scripture! Yet few Bible scholars deny the necessity of being born again in order to get into the kingdom of God.

Actually, the Bible has to mention a matter *only once* for it to be a divine fact. We have more than enough biblical evidence to believe that the second coming is in two phases. The rapture phase will occur prior to the Tribulation, when our Lord calls His church to come up to Himself. The second phase will occur seven years later, at the end of the Tribulation, when Christ comes physically to reign on the earth.

Some critics ridicule pretribulationists by saying that no one passage supports the pretribulation view, and that pretribulationists must take bits and pieces of Scripture and weave them together to come to the pretribulation rapture position. However, I question this allegation because I have found the pretribulation rapture view taught in one verse, in one chapter, and in one book. Let's examine these passages.

The Pretribulation Rapture in One Verse

In Titus 2:13, in the midst of a hard-hitting challenge to God's people to live a holy life, Paul says we should be motivated toward holiness in the anticipation of the second coming of our Lord: "looking for the *blessed hope* and the *glorious appearing* of our great God and Savior Jesus Christ...."

The *blessed hope* is very definitely a reference to the rapture of the church. Examined from every angle, the rapture immediately following the resurrection of dead believers is a "blessed hope." The hope of the church is not to triumph here on this earth, or even be in the majority. Our "hope" or confident expectation is that one day we are going to win in this race called life, not through anything we have done, but because, in accordance with God's mercy, He saves us out of this world before the time of wrath begins.

As I pointed out in the previous chapter, if looking forward to Christ's coming means going through the Tribulation with all its woes, judgments, trumpets, bowls, and catastrophes, it is no "blessed hope" at all. Interestingly enough, in the Bible, the "blessed hope" or rapture is always mentioned in a context of joy.

Consider our Lord's challenge to His disciples the night before He died. He did not say, "Buck up, men; don't let your hearts be troubled just because you have to go through the Tribulation before I can take you to be with myself." Instead, He said, "Let not your heart be troubled.... I will come again and receive you to Myself; that where I am, there you may be also" (John 14:1,3). This is exactly what Paul was referring to when he said, "The Lord Himself will descend.... Then we who are alive and remain shall be caught up...to meet the Lord in the air" (1 Thessalonians 4:16,17). The rapture is truly a *blessed hope* for the church.

The *glorious appearing* is quite a different matter. It is that special day when Christ will be acknowledged by all as "King of kings and

Lord of lords." It is obviously the literal physical stage of His second coming. (Later, we will study a whole chapter about this.)

So, Titus 2:13 shows both phases of the Lord's coming in one verse.

The Pretribulation Rapture in One Chapter

Second Thessalonians 2:1-12 mentions the rapture, Tribulation, and glorious appearing in one chapter. In verse 1, the words "the coming of our Lord Jesus Christ" speak of Christ's return to earth, and is followed by a conjunction that is usually translated "and," but which can also be translated "even." In either case, Paul refers to "our gathering together to Him." The term "second coming" is a reference to the entire coming of Christ, which includes the two phases separated by seven years. The phrase "our gathering together to Him" cannot mean the glorious appearing, since that is when all living creatures are gathered to Him for the judgment of the nations and the establishment of His kingdom. So in verse 1 we have both the glorious appearing and the "gathering together to Him" (the rapture).

Turn now to the next study guide and locate for yourself the events in these 12 verses. (You may want to write lightly so you can list all the events in their proper places, and then, when you finish, go back and darken your writing.)

~ ~ ~

Our Gathering Together to Christ—
2 Thessalonians 2:1-12

Notice what verse 2 says about the day of Christ. What two things must come before that day (verse 3)?

What two names do you find in verse 3 for Antichrist (verse 3)?

List the two things he will do (verse 4).
  1)

  2)

What is Antichrist called in verse 8?

When is he "revealed"?

What will finally happen to him?

When will it happen?

Who will be behind Antichrist (verse 9)?

How do you account for the supernatural signs he will perform during the Tribulation period?

What will the Antichrist do to the unsaved (verse 10)?

Why (verse 10)?

What does God do to the unsaved (verse 11)?

What two reasons are given for this action by God (verse 12)?

1)

2)

In looking back over 2 Thessalonians 2:1-12, you will see that we have the rapture, the Tribulation, and the glorious appearing all in one chapter (study Figure 7 carefully).

~ ~ ~

This is an astonishing thought in Scripture! God is not in the business of sending delusion; He is a revealer of truth. That is why

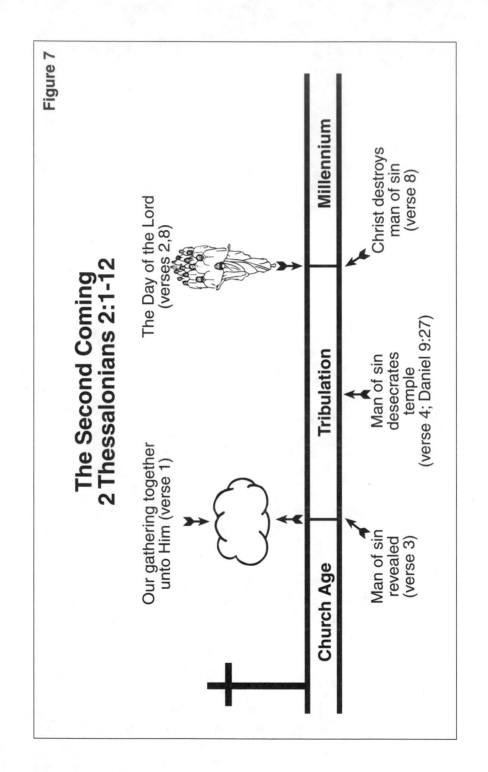

Figure 7

The Second Coming
2 Thessalonians 2:1-12

Our gathering together
unto Him (verse 1)

The Day of the Lord
(verses 2,8)

Church Age

Tribulation

Millennium

Man of sin
revealed
(verse 3)

Man of sin
desecrates
temple
(verse 4; Daniel 9:27)

Christ destroys
man of sin
(verse 8)

He gave us the Bible, His revelation to mankind. He has also given us the Holy Spirit to guide Christians into truth and to convict the unsaved. Yet here we read that God will send a strong delusion so that "they should believe the lie" (verse 11). The lie, of course, will be the Antichrist's gospel, which will be taught by the False Prophet and his followers (Revelation 13).

To understand who the Lord is talking about here, we have to keep in mind Hebrews 11:6, which says, "Without faith it is impossible to please God." During this church age, faith has to be sparked by the Word of God. In Luke 16, Christ quoted Abraham as telling the lost rich man that Lazarus could not go back from the dead to warn the rich man's unbelieving brothers not to come to this place of torment: "They have Moses and the prophets; let them hear them" (verse 29). We have even more: We have the words of Jesus and His apostles. So during the church age it is not by signs and wonders that people are to be saved, but by the preaching of the Word of God.

The people described in 2 Thessalonians 2:9-12 are unsaved people who go into the Tribulation because they heard the gospel, but refused to believe because they "had pleasure in unrighteousness" (verse 12). Doubtless you know individuals who have rejected Christ because they love sin and refuse to give it up to follow Him. If they have heard the Word, they probably know about the rapture. When it occurs, millions of people will be missing on the same day. This obvious miracle will confirm to unbelievers that Scripture is accurate. In addition, during the Tribulation (especially in the first 42 months), unbelievers will see the supernatural signs and wonders done by the two witnesses and hear the testimony of the 144,000 converted Jews. Unbelievers will realize that things are happening just as the Bible said they would. Salvation will not be an act of great faith for them; rather, their response will be based on sight. The signing of the covenant between Israel and the Antichrist will be the signal that they delayed their last chance to accept Christ by faith, and at that point God will send them strong delusion so that they will permanently reject what they know to be true. It is a sad picture, and should motivate us to double our efforts to reach the lost with the gospel while there is still time.

The Pretribulation Rapture in One Book

The book of Revelation was written by John about 50 years after the Lord founded His church and ascended to heaven. In it John not only revealed Jesus Christ in His present and future state, but he also gave an outline of the "things to come." The book begins by describing events in John's day and takes us all the way to the coming of Christ in power and beyond.

Chapter 1 is the introduction, while chapters 2 and 3 cover the church age. Seven historical churches are used to describe the entire church age. For example, the church of Ephesus is the only one that refers to apostles, because that first-century church was the only one that had apostles in it. We do not have space to consider all seven churches here; for that, please see my book *Revelation Unveiled* (Zondervan Publishing House, 1975).

Chapters 4 and 5 describe scenes in heaven. Then, as we have already seen, chapters 6 to 18 give the most detailed description of the events of the Tribulation to be found anywhere in the Bible. In chapter 19 Christ comes physically to the earth and judges the Antichrist, the False Prophet, and the nations. In chapter 20 He binds Satan in the bottomless pit. He then sets up His 1,000-year kingdom on earth, followed by the judgment of the lost of all ages. The last two chapters, 21 and 22, describe the eternal heaven that Christ has prepared for believers of all ages. (Thus the book of Revelation is a chronological description of events from the beginning of the church age all the way to eternity. See Figure 8.)

Again, chapters 2 and 3 of Revelation describe events that will happen on the earth during the church age, while chapters 4 and 5 present a brief description of heaven just prior to the beginning of the Tribulation. Notice what happens to John, a member of the church age, in Revelation 4:1,2:

> After these things I looked, and behold, a door standing open in heaven. And the first voice which I heard was like a trumpet speaking with me, saying, "Come up here, and I will show you things which must take place after this." Immediately I was in the

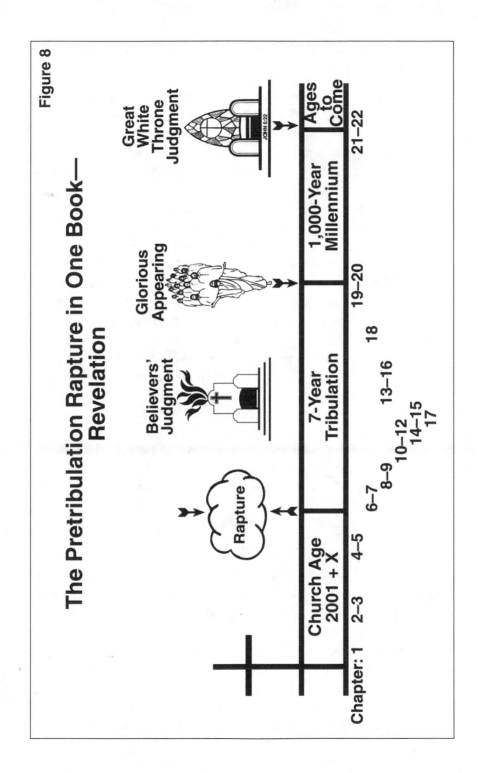

Figure 8

The Pretribulation Rapture in One Book—Revelation

> Spirit; and behold, a throne set in heaven, and One
> sat on the throne.

John is translated from earth to heaven *before* the Tribulation begins. This passage alone does not establish the rapture as a pretribulational event, but in light of the passages we have studied that describe the rapture and the translation of all believers (both dead and living) at this stage of Christ's coming, the fact that John is called up into heaven could certainly serve as a clear implication of the pretribulation rapture. John is at least a symbol of the church when she is raptured to be with Christ "in the air."

As we survey Revelation chapters 4–18, it's vital to observe that we see no mention of the church. In fact, nowhere in the many prophetic passages of Scripture do we see the church in the Tribulation. This is highly significant in view of the passages we have already examined that promise that Christians are saved from wrath.

In the book of Revelation, the church is mentioned *13 times* in the first three chapters. Then, after John is called up into heaven and the world enters the Tribulation, the church is not mentioned even *once* until chapter 19, when she is seen coming with Christ to rule and reign with Him. This silence from chapters 6 to 18 puts the burden of proof on those interpreters who insist that the church does go through all or part of the Tribulation. They should be able to clearly identify the church in Tribulation passages, but they cannot do so.

Summary

The church should not expect to go through Tribulation, although the Jewish people should. They have seven prophetic years still unfulfilled (Daniel's seventieth week), and these years will be fulfilled during that time of wrath called "the time of Jacob's trouble." Unsaved Gentiles will also go through the Tribulation, for their unbelief will prevent them from being raptured.

By contrast, we who are Christians are not looking for that time of wrath. We are looking for the coming of our Lord, and we should so live that if He raptures His church at a time that we don't expect, we will be ready. And certainly every unsaved person who has heard the gospel and understands it should call on the name of the Lord for salvation, lest the rapture come unexpectedly and he be left behind.

More important than any other question on prophecy is this: If Christ comes today to rapture His church, would you be among those who are caught up with Him in the air? If not, you can make yourself ready by personally inviting Christ into your heart by faith.

11

OUR LORD'S OUTLINE
OF PROPHECY

The Olivet Discourse, which was given by our Lord to His disciples on the Mount of Olives the day before His crucifixion, is probably the most important prophetic passage in all the New Testament. The discourse appears in Matthew 24 and 25, Mark 13, and Luke 21. Properly understood, this passage provides a basic outline upon which all other prophetic passages can be located timewise. For that reason we should study it in detail.

Jesus' teaching came about in response to two questions the disciples asked Jesus. They had visited Jerusalem and pointed out to Jesus the temple buildings that had been restored by Herod the Great just a few years before (Matthew 24:1). Evidently Jesus was not as impressed with the building as they were, for He immediately predicted the destruction of that temple. His prophecy was fulfilled less than 40 years later, when the armies of Titus the Roman general surrounded the city, laid a long and torturous siege to it, and finally conquered it. Titus then totally destroyed the city—and the temple.

One interesting sidelight here is that Jesus not only predicted that the temple would be destroyed, but in verse 2 He added, "I say to you, not one stone shall be left here upon another that shall not be thrown down." Today that specific prophecy can be verified by a visit to Jerusalem and the famous "Wailing Wall," which is made of the stones of the temple. Every stone was taken down and removed from the entire temple site, and then some of those same stones were used over a thousand years later to erect what is now called the "Wailing Wall." (This wall is located just off the temple site.) Since the stones are so enormous, each one had to be moved one at a time, thereby fulfilling Christ's prophecy that "there would not be one stone left upon another." This fact has no immediate bearing on the prophecy passage that is about to follow except that it dramatizes the historic accuracy with which our Lord's words were fulfilled. If that one explicit prophecy was fulfilled, we can anticipate that the sweeping panorama of prophecy He was about to give will be equally fulfilled.

≈ ≈ ≈

The Olivet Discourse

After Jesus predicted the destruction of the temple, the disciples asked, "Tell us, when will these things be? And what will be the sign of your coming, and of the end of the age?" (Matthew 24:3). These questions led Jesus to teach the Olivet Discourse. As Jews, the disciples were probably familiar with Daniel 9 and Zechariah 14 and understood that before the coming of Messiah the city of Jerusalem would be surrounded by an enemy army, the city destroyed, and the temple desecrated. Then Messiah would come in great power to set up His kingdom. Their understanding of these prophecies is seen in the questions they asked in Matthew 24:3. Write those questions here:

Matthew 24:3b:

Matthew 24:3c:

What warning did Jesus give in verse 4?

What two deceptions were they to beware of?

    1) (verse 5):

    2) (verse 6a):

What should be the reaction of Christians to "wars and rumors of wars" (verse 6b)?

Why (verse 6c)?

Temporarily skipping the disciples' first question, Jesus began answering their second. What are the four parts of "the sign of Your coming"?

    1) (verse 7a):

    2) (verse 7b):

    3) (verse 7c):

    4) (verse 7d):

~ ~ ~

Evidently, ordinary wars and rumors of wars, which have plagued man for 2,000 years, were not "the sign." A special kind of war would occur that involved many nations, followed by the other three parts of the sign mentioned in verse 7, and this would be "the sign." Can you think of such a war?

Verse 8 is derived from a Hebrew idiom meaning "the beginning of travail" (like birth pains). One pain leads to another, and they increase in intensity until the child is born.

Now read Matthew 24 and locate each event and the verses covered by it as best you can on Figure 9. Include also the events covered in Matthew 25:31-46. Do not look at my end-of-chapter chart (Figure 10) for comparison until you have designed your own chart! Then compare them. If you have difficulty locating an event, move on to the next section and return to the unfinished sections later.

One thing you will discover here is that because the disciples had no understanding of the rapture, and because the events Jesus described (except for the signs) will occur after the rapture, it is not mentioned in this passage. Our Lord's view here was primarily of what would happen to *Israel* at the end of the age. However, we can be certain of the rapture based on other Bible passages we examined earlier. Go ahead and mark, on Figure 9, where you think the rapture will occur, using a dotted line.

When the disciples asked their two questions, note that they merged together the glorious appearing of Messiah, whom the Orthodox Jews to this day expect to come in glorious power, destroying the enemies of Israel, and then setting up the future kingdom promised by many Old Testament prophets.

Our Lord warned His disciples to take heed that they not be deceived by false messiahs. He knew that many false messiahs would come, deceiving many (and they have), but they are not *the sign*. Then He injected the subject of war, but said that *the sign* was not just an ordinary war, like the hundreds that have occurred since He left this world. Instead, He predicted that there would be a special kind of war beginning with one nation rising against another until they were joined by the kingdoms of the world. But even that is not

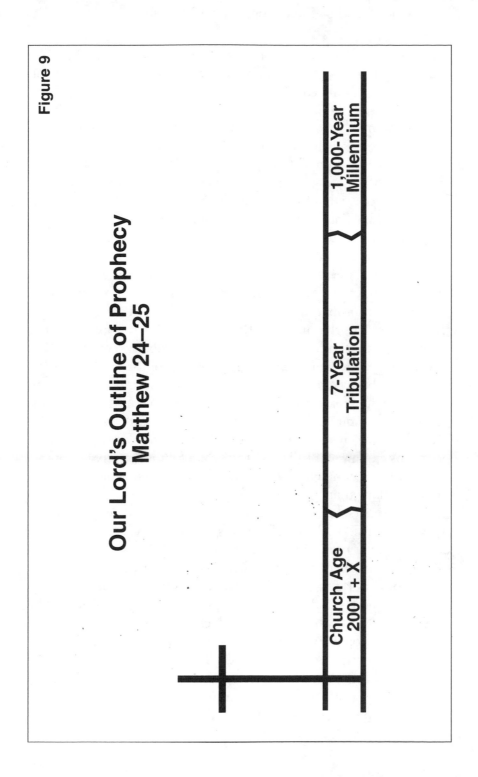

Figure 9

Our Lord's Outline of Prophecy
Matthew 24–25

Church Age
2001 + X

7-Year
Tribulation

1,000-Year
Millennium

the entire sign. That was just the first portion of a sign, which, if followed by famines, pestilence, and earthquakes in various places at the same time would comprise the "beginning of sorrows" (verse 8).

Here, Jesus used an interesting idiom, referring to the first birth pain of a woman giving birth. The first birth pain is followed by others, and eventually they increase in number and become more intense until "the end." Other signs regarding the end of the age and the Lord's coming are given in several other Scripture passages. For a detailed study of these many signs, please see my book *The Beginning of the End* (Tyndale House Publishers, 1981).

Before we get to the subsequent events, I should point out that historically there has been only one event that comes close to fulfilling all these signs—World War I, which was followed by unprecedented famines, pestilences, and earthquakes. But this alone does not mean that it was *the sign*, although many Christians thought for years that it was. Early in the twentieth century, Jewish people began returning to Israel in larger numbers, especially with the signing of the Balfour Treaty in 1916 as promised in Ezekiel 36, and Russia became a dominant world power (starting in 1917) as prophesied in Ezekiel 38 and 39, and other seeming fulfillments began to occur during World War I. However, Matthew 24:34 indicates that the generation that sees the fulfillment of *the sign* "will by no means pass away till all these things are fulfilled." Very few of the people who saw the First World War are still alive, which makes it rather unlikely that World War I was "the sign." As long as some of those old-timers, born around 1900, still remain, the interpretation of World War I as "the sign" remains a possibility, but at present it doesn't seem as probable as it once did.

On the other hand, it could be that these events were just a sample of a world war that will yet fulfill all the requirements of "the sign," thereby indicating that it is near. That could conceivably be World War III, which, God forbid, could come in our lifetime.

Another popular view held by many students of prophecy is that the fig tree mentioned in Matthew 24:32 is "the sign." They suggest that since the fig tree, when used symbolically, refers to Israel, then the regathering of Israel is the sign. Matthew 24:7 could then be "the beginning of sorrows" or the first birth pain of the sign, although verse 32 is really *the sign*. They point out that although some Jews were in the land prior to World War I, it took the signing of the Balfour Treaty in 1916 to cause thousands of Jews to begin gathering back into the land of Israel, and that the fulfillment of this sign occurred in 1948 when Israel was recognized as a sovereign country by the United Nations. If so, then there is plenty of time remaining during which the "generation" of Matthew 24:34 that saw Israel established as a nation could still be alive, or "by no means pass away till all these things are fulfilled." That could be another 40 years or so.

You may wonder at all this ambiguity regarding "the sign" and which generation will be alive when the Lord comes. (Remember that the disciples, too, just like ourselves, were interested in "the sign of Christ's coming.") But our Lord warned them, "Of that day and hour no one knows, no, not even the angels of heaven, but My Father only" (Matthew 24:36). It is not God's will that we know the day or the hour! That is why date-setters can always be branded as wrong. We simply cannot predict the time of Christ's return. Those who attempt to do so bring unnecessary embarrassment on the church. However, as Jesus indicated in the parable of the fig tree, it is possible to know, based on indications that the signs are falling into place, "that summer is near" (Matthew 24:32). That is, they can know that the "season" for Christ's return is approaching.

Ours may not be the generation that participates in the rapture—yet again it could be. Why? Because our generation has more prophetic reason, through fulfilled prophecy, to believe that Christ is coming than any generation since Christ ascended and promised to return.

Now let's turn back to what happens next after *the sign.* Matthew 24:9 introduces the Tribulation and subsequent events. In the verses that follow, you will find information that parallels our previous studies of that seven-year period. Let's take a closer look at these verses.

≈ ≈ ≈

Matthew 24–25

Have verses 9-14 ever been fulfilled in history?

List five things that will happen during the first half of the Tribulation.

1)

2)

3)

4)

5)

What good news is found in verse 14?

Verse 15 mentions a very important event. Read Daniel 9:27, 11:31, and 12:11, which are parallel verses, and then describe the event. Add this event to your chart on page 109.

What does Jesus tell the Jews living at that time to do (verses 16-20)?

What does our Lord call this new phase of the tribulation period (verse 21)?

List some of the characteristics of that age as described in verses 21-26.

What does verse 27 tell us about Christ's second coming?

List five miracles that will happen when Christ returns (verses 29,30a).

   1)

   2)

   3)

   4)

   5)

Why do the "tribes mourn" (verse 30)?

Describe what will happen to "the elect" of verse 31.

What can we know according to the parable of the fig tree (verses 32,33)? What does verse 36 say?

What is Christ teaching in verses 37-39 and 40-44?

What is His conclusion (verses 45-47)?

What happens to those who reject Him (verses 48-51)?

Briefly summarize the judgment of the nations as described in Matthew 25:31-46.

≈ ≈ ≈

We have already seen that our Lord's Olivet Discourse in Matthew 24–25 is the most important passage of prophecy in the New Testament. If you understand this passage you will be able to determine the timing of most of the events in other Bible prophecies. Matthew 24:9-31 provides the essential details of the Tribulation period right up to the second coming of Christ to the earth to set up His literal, physical kingdom. This is amazingly compatible with Revelation chapters 6 to 19 and 2 Thessalonians 2:1-12, which we have already studied.

You will recall that the disciples asked the Lord, "What will be the sign of Your coming, and of the end of the age?" They merged the two events together because at that point they had never been told about the rapture of the church. So the Lord gave them the sign, which, as we have seen, will be a monstrous world war followed by famines, pestilences, and earthquakes. Then He called that event the "beginning of sorrows" or the first birth pain. This symbolizes a process of time interspersed by several other "birth pains" or events of history that fulfill prophecy. Matthew 24:9 then introduces what follows that sign without giving the length of it. Then in verse 32, where Christ takes up the subject of the sign again, He tells the parable of the fig tree (which may refer to the establishment of Israel) and warns the disciples that when these things take place, "summer is near," "at the very doors."

Admittedly, this is a complex and difficult passage to understand. But the best interpretation seems to be that of taking the phrase "This generation [that sees this sign] will by no means pass away till all these things are fulfilled" (verse 34) to mean that the generation that sees the special war mentioned in verse 7 will not pass away until the Tribulation and the glorious appearing "are fulfilled."

As I mentioned earlier, there are some who believe the sign of Christ's coming, as described in Matthew 24:6,7, was World War I. However, the generation that saw the First World War of 1914–1918 (which was, interestingly enough, followed by famines, pestilences, and earthquakes) has almost vanished from the earth. Not very many people who can remember the events of 1914–1918 are still alive. They would be around 90 years old today. However, Christ said they would see "*all* these things fulfilled," which would include the seven-year tribulation period. So we must add another seven years to their age, making them nearly 100 years old. Every day that passes finds fewer of that generation still alive. Consequently, although the interpretation of World War I as "the sign" is still possible, it has become increasingly unlikely.

If, on the other hand, verse 7 is just describing the fact that the 2,000 years of present history would be filled with war after war, along with famines, pestilences, and earthquakes, but that the fig tree parable, which supposedly began with the Balfour Treaty and culminated with the 1948 establishment of the nation of Israel, is really *the sign*, then another 30 to 40 (or more) years can be added to allow time for "the generation that sees all these things."

Whichever interpretation is taken is not nearly so important as the fact that the coming of Christ for His church could very well be near, "even at the very doors" (Matthew 24:33). This truth should affect the way we live! More important than *when* Christ comes is the fact that He *is* coming and that Christians should be *ready* for Him when He arrives.

After Christ comes to receive His own (Matthew 24:9), the Tribulation begins here on earth (or at least that portion of the Tribulation covered in Revelation 6 and 7, after the world leader makes a covenant with Israel for seven years yet breaks it after three-and-a-half years). During the Tribulation, believers will experience difficult days of opposition, false Christs, and lawlessness. But the gospel of the kingdom will be preached around the world, probably by the 144,000 Jewish witnesses of Revelation 7, who will reach "a great multitude which no one [can] number, of all nations, tribes, peoples, and tongues" (Revelation 7:9).

Matthew 24:15 portrays the "abomination of desolation," or the Antichrist's desecration of the rebuilt temple in Jerusalem. The fact that he will desecrate it tells us the temple will have to be rebuilt either before or in the first few years of the Tribulation. That desecration comes in the middle of the Tribulation and triggers what our Lord called the "Great Tribulation" (Matthew 24:21), which will be the worst time in the history of the world for Christians who refuse

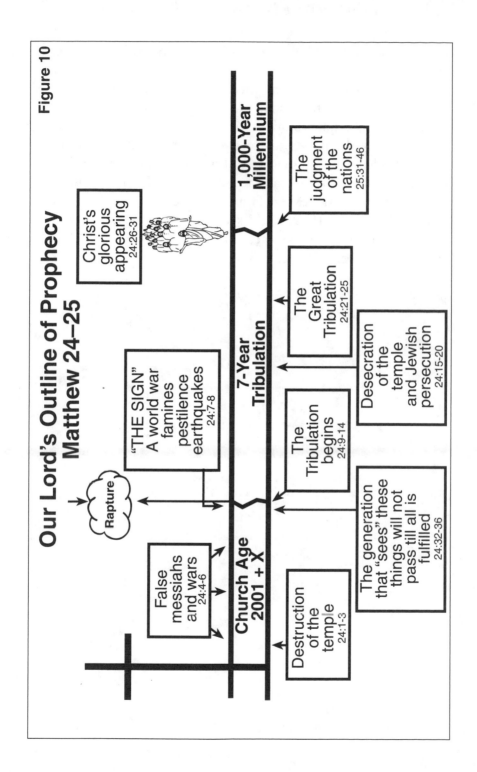

Figure 10

to bow down and worship "the beast" or the one-world government leader called Antichrist.

The seven-year Tribulation will culminate with the coming of Christ in power to establish His kingdom on earth—which we have yet to study. The important message of our Lord to everyone here, and especially the church, is to live a holy life and be ready for whenever He comes, so that we will not have any regrets when we face Him. Jesus said, "Be ready, for the Son of Man is coming at an hour when you do not expect Him" (Matthew 24:44). He also said, "Occupy *till I come*" (Luke 19:13 KJV, emphasis added).

Study the chart in Figure 10 carefully and compare it with the chart you created in Figure 9.

12

THE GLORIOUS APPEARING

The most thrilling event in all of human history is yet to come. It will be that moment in time when our Lord Jesus Christ returns to this earth in power and great glory to set up His kingdom that will last 1,000 years. From a prophetic standpoint, it will be the culmination of all prophecy. Nearly 325 prophecies that speak of Christ's second coming guarantee it will take place and will usher in the most idealistic conditions on earth since the garden of Eden.

Words seem inadequate to fully describe that magnificent event that will combine all the hopes and dreams of the billions of people who have put their faith in God from Adam and Eve to the end of the Tribulation. What will Christ look like? No one knows. For although hundreds of pictures of Him have been painted and circulated, they are all just mere human thoughts of what He might look like. The only way I know to describe Him is He will be magnificent! He will appear as God in human flesh, and He will look like He did when He was on this earth. But He will also appear in a glorified body and be worshiped by both angels and men. One thing is certain: He will not appear as the suffering servant that He was the first time He came. The next time He comes, and for all eternity, He will be in His glorified state.

While no one knows what Christ will look like when He returns, we do have many descriptions of what He will do when He

119

comes. To get a full picture, we must turn to several prophecies and put them all together. We will start with Jesus' own description of His second coming and the incredible events that will trigger.

Christ's Coming Attended by Signs and Natural Phenomena

In Matthew 24:29-31, Jesus said, "Immediately after the tribulation of those days the sun will be darkened, and the moon will not give its light; the stars will fall from heaven, and the powers of the heavens will be shaken. Then the sign of the Son of Man will appear in heaven, and then all·the tribes of the earth will mourn, and they will see the Son of Man coming on the clouds of heaven with power and great glory. And He will send His angels with a sound of a trumpet, and they will gather His elect from the four winds, from one end of heaven to the other."

This prediction of our Lord Himself concerning His glorious appearing is taken from the Olivet Discourse. It reveals that He will come visibly and become the object of attention. The sun, moon, and stars will not give their lights, but all attention will be focused on "the sign of the Son of Man [that] will appear in heaven," after which "all the tribes of the earth will mourn" because they have not prepared themselves for that day. Then all people will see Christ, who is the Light, "coming on the clouds of heaven with power and great glory." At this moment the second installment of the rapture will occur, when Christ gathers together "His elect from the four winds, from one end of heaven to the other."

Christ Comes to Execute Judgment with His Saints

Enoch, the seventh from Adam, prophesied: "Behold, the Lord comes with ten thousands of his saints, to execute judgment on all, to convict all who are ungodly among them of all their ungodly deeds which they have committed in an ungodly way, and of all the harsh things which ungodly sinners have spoken against him" (Jude 14,15).

This is the only passage in the Bible that informs us that Enoch was a prophet. Somehow God had revealed to him that one day,

Christ would come with myriad holy ones to execute judgment on humankind. That judgment will begin with Antichrist and will eventually include the nations of the earth, as explained in Matthew 25. Second Thessalonians 2:7-10 describes Christ's coming in judgment to destroy Antichrist by casting him into the lake of fire.

Christ Will Stand on the Mount of Olives

Zechariah 14:3-5 prophesies: "The LORD will go forth and fight against those nations, as He fights in the day of battle. And in that day His feet will stand on the Mount of Olives, which faces Jerusalem on the east, and the Mount of Olives shall be split in two, from east to west, making a very large valley; half of the mountain shall move toward the north and half of it toward the south. Then you shall flee through My mountain valley, for the mountain shall reach to Azal. Yes, you shall flee as you fled from the earthquake in the days of Uzziah king of Judah. Thus the LORD my God will come, and all the saints with you" (Zechariah 14:3-5).

Our Lord ascended into heaven from the Mount of Olives. In Acts 1:11 the angels said, "This same Jesus, who was taken up from you into heaven, will so come in like manner as you saw Him go into heaven." Our Lord will not only come "in like manner," meaning visibly and physically, but He will actually come to the same place, the Mount of Olives. When His feet strike the Mount of Olives, that hill will divide in two.

Christ Will Come as King of Kings

Of all the descriptions of the glorious appearing in the Bible, none is more graphic than that foreseen by the apostle John:

> Then I saw heaven opened, and behold, a white horse. And He who sat on him was called Faithful and True, and in righteousness He judges and makes war. His eyes were like a flame of fire, and on His head were many crowns. He had a name written that no one knew except Himself. He was clothed with a robe dipped in blood, and His name is called the

> Word of God. And the armies in heaven, clothed in fine linen, white and clean, followed Him on white horses. Now out of His mouth goes a sharp sword, that with it He should strike the nations. And He Himself will rule them with a rod of iron. He Himself treads the winepress of the fierceness and wrath of Almighty God. And He has on His robe and on His thigh a name written: King of kings and Lord of lords (Revelation 19:11-16).

Verse 11 introduces this dynamic scene by telling us that John sees "heaven opened." This is the second time John has seen heaven opened. The first time was in Revelation 4:1, where he was invited up into heaven and, as a representative of the church, looked down on the scenes of the Tribulation. In Revelation chapter 19 the Tribulation has been concluded and Christ is returning to earth, so we find heaven opened again. This time, instead of taking a man up, heaven is opened to let the rider on the white horse out, accompanied by His armies.

This rider is to be distinguished from the rider on the white horse in Revelation 6:2, who will be the Antichrist. The present rider, with eyes "like a flame of fire," can be none other than the Lord Jesus Christ. The significance of the white horse is typical of the difference between this coming and Christ's first coming. While on this earth our Lord fulfilled Zechariah 9:9, entering Jerusalem humbly on a lowly beast of burden. Now His humiliation is done away with and He will come in glory, properly using a white horse, a symbol of victory, power, and glory.

Even more significant than what our Lord will do at His coming is how He is described—here, we see His eternal nature revealed. "Faithful and True" presents our Lord as a contrast of the unfaithful deceivers of humankind, Antichrist and Satan. At the time of His return, our Lord will have faithfully fulfilled all of His prophecies up to that point, and "in righteousness" He will mete out judgment (Revelation 19:11).

When Christ comes as the righteous warrior, He will be invincible. He will consume all before Him, all that stand in opposition to Him, and bring every person into subjection to Himself. At His return, we will witness the first clearly righteous war in the history of humankind. The ability of Christ to wage a righteous war is not only seen in His holy nature, but in that His eyes are "like a flame of fire," indicating that He will judge according to truth. The best judge on earth cannot know all the facts of a given situation because he or she is limited by human frailty. Jesus Christ is not so limited. He who knows the end from the beginning will be a righteous judge, for His all-seeing eyes will reveal all truth about every individual and nation.

Christ Will Return as the Righteous King

Revelation 19:12 tells us that when Christ returns, He will have many crowns on His head. This means He will come as one with sovereign authority. All through history a crown on a person's head has symbolized authority. Kings wore crowns, the popes wear a triple crown, the Antichrist's kingdom is symbolized in Scripture with crowns, and even the ten kings of the Tribulation will have crowns. But when Christ comes, all power will be given to Him as the Supreme King. In fact, Revelation 19:11-12 reveals a threefold nature of Christ at His glorious appearing: He will come as a judge, a warrior, and a king.

Revelation 19:12 adds that Christ will have on Him "a name written that no one knew except Himself." Many have speculated about this name, but it seems unwise to do so. In the Bible, a name reveals the nature of the person, and in Scripture, there are many names that reveal various facets of the nature of God and Jesus Christ. However, since Jesus is divine, it seems only natural that some aspects of His nature are incomprehensible to our finite minds. Therefore at least this one name will be unknown to us.

Verse 13 goes on to say that when Christ returns, He will be dressed in a robe dipped in blood. This may well be a reference to the bloodshed caused by the battle of the great Day of God Almighty as He triumphs over all who oppose Him.

The Lord Will Return with His Armies

Revelation 19:14 describes for us who will appear with Christ at His glorious appearing: "The armies of heaven, clothed in fine linen, white and clean, followed Him on white horses." The armies of heaven consist of the angelic hosts, the Old Testament saints, the church, and the Tribulation saints. Note especially the garb of this army: fine linen, white and clean. Military men are issued colored uniforms for battle dress—not only for camouflage purposes, but also because fighting a war gets a soldier so dirty that white clothes would be severely soiled. Here, however, the Commander-in-Chief of the heavenly forces clothes His army in white, a practice unheard of in the history of warfare. That's because no member of the armies of Christ will do battle! Not one of us will lift a finger, for the battle will be consummated by the spoken word of our Lord Himself.

The Authority of the King of Kings

In Revelation 19:15 we read this: "Out of his mouth goes a sharp sword, that with it He should strike the nations. And He Himself will rule them with a rod of iron." Christ will come victorious, and strike down His enemies. Christ's glorious appearing with the heavenly armies will not only bring to consummation the enmity of Satan, his Antichrist, the False Prophet, and the millions they deceive, but it will also usher in the righteous reign of Christ on earth. This fact is seen clearly in the name given to Christ in verse 16: "On His robe and on His thigh a name [is] written: King of kings and Lord of lords" (Revelation 19:16).

A warrior goes into battle with his sword on his thigh; Christ's sword will be His spoken word. The word that called the world into being will call human leaders and the armies of all nations into control. And Christ Jesus, the living Lord, will be established in that day for what He is in reality: King above all kings, Lord above all lords. The prophet Zechariah said it best: "And the LORD shall be king over all the earth. In that day shall be—the LORD is one, and His name one." Amen!

13

THE CHRISTIAN RESURRECTION FROM THE DEAD

Belief in life after death is not unique to Christianity. It is so ingrafted into human intuition that nearly every religion in the world is built on that expectation—as though the Creator wanted man to know that once born, human beings are eternal. From the primitive tribesmen of the jungles to the sophisticated Oriental mystics, virtually every tradition has some system of belief in the afterlife.

For some people, like the American Indians, it is just another life in "the happy hunting grounds." For others, such as Hindus, it is a complex series of afterlives in a higher or lower caste system here on earth, depending on how a person lived. The good come back in a higher caste; the bad come back in a lower one. The Parsis of India wear masks over their mouths so they won't swallow a gnat and by chance inhale their grandfather, who happened to be such a degenerate that he came back in the bug caste.

Christianity tells without doubt the most beautiful story of life in the afterlife—for believers. Our Bible gives far more interesting and believable details about the next life than any other religion. That should not be surprising, since only Christianity has a Bible that came from God Himself, some parts of which were revealed personally by His own Son, who said, "I have come that they may have life, and that they may have it more abundantly" (John 10:10).

125

To get an idea of how much the Old Testament Scriptures speak of a bodily resurrection, answer the questions that follow.

≈ ≈ ≈

The Old Testament Teaching on Resurrection

Job was the first person to record a biblical reference to the resurrection. He is considered to be the most knowledgeable man in the first 2,000 years of recorded history regarding the ways of God. Study Job 19:25-27, and answer the following questions.

What two things did Job know about God (verse 25)?

In what condition did Job expect to see God after his death (verse 26)?

What would be his relationship to God at the time (verse 27)?

Abraham, the father of the Hebrew race and quite possibly the most venerated of all the Old Testament patriarchs (since more space is given to him in the New Testament than to any other Old Testament leader), must have believed in bodily resurrection.

In the book of Hebrews, the Holy Spirit reveals that Abraham looked for something after death. What was it (11:10)?

In what state did he believe life would be in the next world (11:19)?

King David, the psalm writer, lived about 1,000 years before Christ and described his beliefs about the next life. Study Psalm 16:7-11.

How did David face death (verse 9)?

What did he say in verse 10?

What did he expect in the future (verse 11)?

Would that be possible without resurrection?

Daniel, one of the greatest and most righteous men in the Bible, said what of death in Daniel 12:2?

How does he describe "awake"?

Let's consider the Jewish view at the time of Christ: In John 11:24, Martha, the sister of Lazarus (whom Jesus raised from the dead), reflected the view of her generation. What was it?

To this day the Jews hold the same view that Martha expressed to Jesus. Is that statement compatible with the Christian view?

≈ ≈ ≈

Summary

Christianity is a religion of resurrection. Our Lord gave His own resurrection as the paramount sign of His deity (Matthew 12:39). His disciples, a defeated lot after His crucifixion, were motivated to world evangelism by His resurrection. In fact, all of them except John were martyred for their testimony that they had personally seen Christ alive after His resurrection. Not only the apostles saw Him, but, as Luke said, "He presented Himself alive after His suffering by many infallible proofs" (Acts 1:3) over a period of 40 days after His resurrection. On one occasion He was seen by 120 people in the upper room, and at another time (possibly His ascension) He was seen by about 500 people at once (1 Corinthians 15:6). It was the fact of the resurrection that motivated these disciples and apostles to "turn the world upside down" by their Spirit-empowered evangelism and the testimony that the angels gave: "He is not here; for He is risen, as He said" (Matthew 28:6).

In addition, Christ taught on several occasions that the graves of believers would open and come forth to "everlasting life" (See John 5:21,24 as just one example). In John 11, just prior to raising Lazarus from the dead (the third person Jesus raised), Christ distinctly tied

Himself to the fact of resurrection with these words: "I am the resurrection and the life. He who believes in Me, though he may die, he shall live. And whoever lives and believes in Me shall never die" (John 11:25,26).

Without question, it is impossible to remove Jesus Christ from resurrection. It is a doctrinal necessity in that if there is no resurrection, Christianity is a fraud; Christ would not be divine, and, as Paul said, "You are still in your sins" (1 Corinthians 15:17). But because Christ *did* rise from the dead, we have His promise, "Because I live, you will live also" (John 14:19).

≈ ≈ ≈

The Christian View of Resurrection
1 Corinthians 15

How important to Christianity is the resurrection of the body?

Verse 13:

Verse 14a:

Verse 14b:

Verse 15a:

Verse 15b:

Verse 16:

Verse 17:

Verse 18:

If there is no resurrection, what are we (verse 19)?

There are distinct orders of resurrection. What are they?

Verses 20,23a:

Verse 23b:

Verse 24:

∼ ∼ ∼

The Resurrected Body
1 Corinthians 15

Why is our present body unable to go right to heaven or the millennial kingdom (15:35-42)?

Verse 43:

What kind of body will our resurrected body be (verse 44)?

Does this mean it will not be a real body that is recognizable or can talk? See Colossians 3:4.

First Corinthians 15:47-49 gives more details. What are they?

Why must our body be changed (verse 50)?

What is Paul's "mystery" (verses 51-53)?

≈ ≈ ≈

Resurrection Before Rapture

When Christ comes to rapture His church, two kinds of Christians will be raptured. Can you identify them? Compare 1 Corinthians 15:52 and 1 Thessalonians 4:13a.

Who does Paul refer to in 4:14b?

Who does Paul talk about in 4:15a?

What about in 4:15b?

Summarize the two classes of Christians you find in 1 Thessalonians 4:13-15.

    1)

    2)

What will *not* happen (verse 15)?

What is the one condition required to be a part of this resurrection (4:14)?

What is that called in 1 Corinthians 15:1-3?

≈ ≈ ≈

Old Testament Saints and Tribulation Saints

The Bible is not entirely clear on whether Old Testament saints will be included in the rapture. Some believe the rapture is only for the church, and that Old Testament believers who looked forward to the cross by faith will remain in the grave until the glorious appearing. That may account for the fact that the Old Testament saints are not specifically mentioned in any rapture passage. The rapture may be for the church only, which would fit the overall plan of God's dealing with Israel in the Old Testament, as separate from His dealing specifically with the church for almost 2,000 years in the present church age. (Then, during the seven years of the Tribulation at the end of history, He will go back to leading Israel in a personal way. Then, at the end of the Tribulation, God will resurrect the dead Old Testament saints and the Tribulation saints, who will be joined together with the church to go with Christ into the millennium.)

The resurrection-rapture of the Old Testament saints may be what the psalmist foresaw in Psalm 50. There, the Messiah is seen in the air calling back to heaven for the Old Testament saints and the believers who died during the Tribulation. Then He gathers those on earth to Him by changing their mortal bodies as He comes to earth in His glorious appearing (Psalm 50:4,5). This would account for the resurrection of all believers of all time to that point. (The *millennial* saints will be resurrected and changed 1,000 years later.)

Summary

The Bible teaches that our present body is "corruptible" (1 Corinthians 15:53,54)—that is, it is human or "natural." That is why we can still sin after we have been born again. At salvation, God's Spirit comes into our heart so that at the time of death our soul (the eternal part of our being) and our "new nature" or "spirit" departs to be with Christ, where it remains until the resurrection-rapture. Then when Christ descends from heaven "with a shout... and the dead in Christ will rise first. Then we who are alive and remain shall be caught up together with them in the clouds" (1 Thessalonians 4:16,17). Then we shall all "meet the Lord in the air" and be with Him forever.

Those believers who happen to be alive on earth when Christ comes in the air will also be "changed" in the rapture. Our bodies, like those of fellow believers before us who "are asleep in Jesus," are unfit for heaven and must be changed like Christ's body was after His resurrection. That future heavenly body will be made from the elements of our present bodies, or our former bodies, in the case of dead believers. (Wherever these bodies are—in the ocean, the grave, etc.—they will be resurrected.) Elements are never lost; God can gather each body's elements from any place in the universe no matter where they are on resurrection day, and He can reunite them with the soul and spirit forever.

This new, resurrected body, made from the elements of our former body, will be recognizable, will be able to communicate with other saints, and will even be able to eat, for our Lord ate fish with His disciples after His resurrection. Yet His resurrected body was not subject to time or space; He could walk through walls and travel great distances at the speed of thought. In this state we will be with the Lord forever. It is in this immortal body that we will rule with Christ throughout the millennium, and after that go into heaven for the eternity to come.

You can ransack the libraries of the world, but you'll never find a religion that offers a more complete and inspiring description of future life than that found in the "blessed hope" that God has prepared for those who love Him and have put their faith in His Son. This is what the Bible calls "the first resurrection."

I want to ask you two important questions:

1) Will you be a part of that resurrection? You need to answer that question for yourself.

2) If you are a Christian, are you living the kind of life that Christ expects of you in preparation for either death or His coming?

Note: Locate, with a dotted line, the resurrection of the believing dead (when Christ comes in the rapture) on Figure 11.

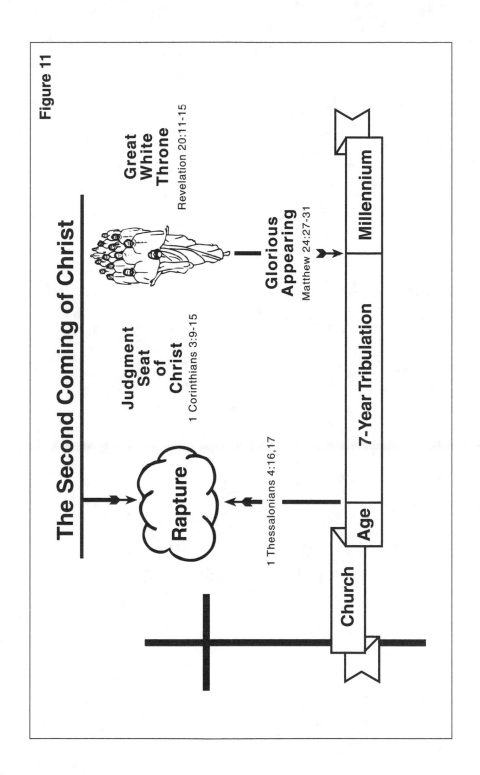

Figure 11

14

WHEN RESURRECTED CHRISTIANS MEET THEIR LORD

Most Christians look forward to that incredible day when they will see their Lord. As we have already seen, God's plan for us, according to 1 Thessalonians 4:16,17, is to meet our dead loved ones and friends "in the clouds" first, then to meet the Lord "in the air."

Preachers have waxed eloquent describing both of those meetings. Like many Christians, I have two parents I long to meet in the clouds, along with many friends. But even that ecstatic moment will be eclipsed in the ecstasy of actually meeting the Lord who died for us, forgave us, saved us, led us through life, and resurrected us. Words cannot suffice to adequately describe that scene!

However, immediately after that event we will be judged by Him! Few Christians ever think about that. First Corinthians 4:5 says, "Judge nothing before the appointed time; wait till the Lord comes. He will bring to light what is hidden in darkness and will expose the motives of men's hearts" (NIV). Obviously, when the Lord comes, He is going to judge His servants by examining their works and motives.

This meeting with our Lord in judgment is not an obscure teaching in Scripture. Keep in mind, however, that this judgment is not for the purpose of determining whether or not we are saved, nor is it a judgment for sins committed prior to our salvation, for those sins were judged by God at Calvary when Christ died for those sins and were forgiven the moment we confessed them (1 John 1:9). Instead, this judgment is to determine the rewards that we will receive for our faithful service after our salvation. But it's time for you to study this for yourself. Please answer the following study questions.

~ ~ ~

Christians at the Judgment of Reward

What is this judgment called (Romans 14:10)?

Who will stand before the Judge (14:12)?

What do you think "give account" means?

What is this judgment called in 2 Corinthians 5:10?

Who will stand at that judgment?

What is this judgment for (5:12c)?

So what should be our conclusion (5:9)?

The most detailed description of this judgment for believers is found in 1 Corinthians 3:9-15. Locate the timing of this judgment on the chart in Figure 12.

≈ ≈ ≈

The Judgment of Reward
1 Corinthians 3:9-15

What does Paul call Christians in verse 9?

Who laid the foundation (verses 10,11)?

What do you think that means?

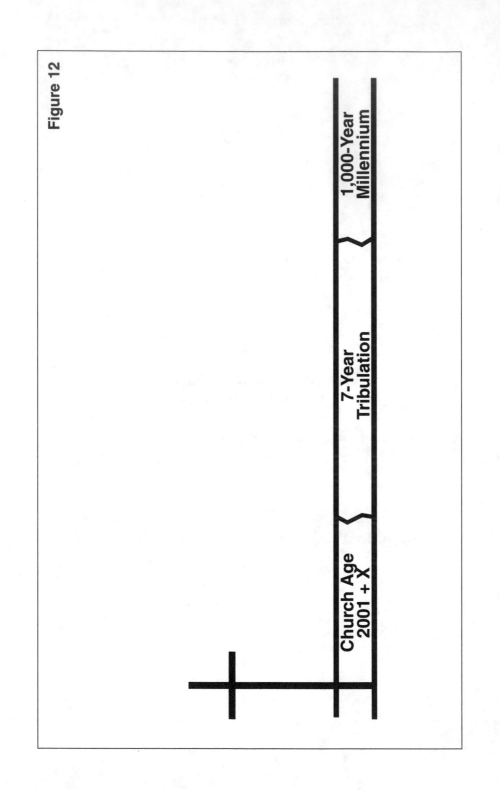

Figure 12

Church Age
2001 + X

7-Year
Tribulation

1,000-Year
Millennium

List the six symbols Paul uses for good works in verse 12.

1)

2)

3)

4)

5)

6)

What will test those works (verse 13b)?

When (verse 13b)?

What will it test for (verse 13c)?

What happens if a believer's works survive the test (verse 14)?

What happens if they don't (verse 15)?

How would that believer be saved (verse 15b)?

What does that mean?

Write your own summary of this passage before reading onward.

～ ～ ～

The Misconception About Good Works

Because we are saved "by grace...through faith, and that not of yourselves; it is the gift of God, not of works, lest anyone should boast" (Ephesians 2:8,9), many Christians think there is little or no call on their life to serve our Lord. Consequently they accept His salvation as a gift and do nothing to advance His kingdom. Unfortunately, they do not read on to the following verse: "We are His workmanship, created in Christ Jesus for good works, which God prepared beforehand that we should walk in them" (Ephesians 2:10).

It is obvious from this passage that the Lord expects His children to work for Him after they have been given salvation. In fact, we will be rewarded in the next life in direct proportion to the way we have served Him in this one.

~ ~ ~

What Are Good Works?

What type of "good work" is mentioned in Matthew 5:16?

What kind is mentioned in Matthew 26:7-10?

What does "rich in good works" mean (1 Timothy 6:18)?

Can only the rich perform good works (Matthew 10:42)?

What does Christ consider a good work (Matthew 10:40-42)?

What happens to those who do such works (verse 42c)?

    Such challenges are not uncommon in our Lord's teachings; often, they appear in His parables. Bible scholars define a parable as "an earthly story with a heavenly meaning." Since few of Jesus' listeners could imagine the kingdom of heaven, which believers will occupy during the millennium or "kingdom age," Jesus used stories they could understand so that they and we could better understand what He was saying. Read the parables below and give a brief summary of each one.

Parable of the talents (Matthew 25:14-30):

Parable of the pounds (Luke 19:11-27):

Parable of the wages (Matthew 20:1-16):

What similarities do you find between these parables?

What differences are there in the rewards?

What do you learn from Matthew 20:1-16 about the relationship between rewards and the length of time a believer has in this life to serve the Lord?

∽ ∽ ∽

Summary of Judgment of Reward

Although the gift of salvation is freely given by a generous God, we are expected, once saved, to serve our Lord by doing good works. A good work can be anything done in the name of the Lord or for His glory. It could be witnessing, worshiping Him, or even giving a cup of cold water to someone.

The symbolism in these parables we just examined is interesting in that Jesus compares Himself to a "householder" (landowner) or even a king who went on a long journey and, after a "great while" (almost 2,000 years?), returned—at which time he demanded of his servants an accounting and gave rewards according to their faithfulness, talent, and time spent in labor.

Talent + Gospel + Time = Reward

My formula for this reward is this: *Talent* times our productive sharing of the *gospel* times the amount of *time* we had after our salvation to labor will equal our *reward*. The record of our works is kept by God, who knows what ability we have to serve Him and will hold us accountable for how we use our talents and time for service. Fortunately, He is a just God and will treat each believer "according to what he has done" (2 Corinthians 5:10), based on his or her natural ability.

Our Lord challenged us:

> Do not lay up for yourselves treasures on earth, where moth and rust destroy and where thieves break in and steal; but lay up for yourselves treasures in heaven, where neither moth nor rust destroys and where thieves do not break in and steal. For where your treasure is, there your heart will be also (Matthew 6:19-21).

God, in His mercy, has not only given us the free gift of salvation, but He also gives us an opportunity to invest a portion of our "treasure" (our life) in eternal rewards. It seems that when we are saved, our Lord opens for us a bank account in heaven. All through our life we can deposit into that account "treasure" or "good works" done in His name and for His glory. Then when He comes we will stand before Him as He opens that account to see how much we have invested. He then will test it "by fire" to see how genuine it is.

According to 1 Corinthians 3:12,13, some of these works will be gold, silver, or precious jewels, meaning that they will survive the fire and the believer will receive a reward. (The rewards will be covered in a later summary.) But the works that comprise wood, hay, and stubble will not survive the fire, and those believers will suffer loss of reward—not loss of salvation, but loss of *reward*. They will be saved "so as by fire," or as we might say, "by the skin of their teeth." They will be saved, but their works will be lost.

Bad Works That Are Burned Up

The works that won't survive the fire are those that were not done with the right spirit or motive. To the eyes of man they may look like silver, gold, and precious stones, but in reality they are nothing but wood, hay, and stubble. God's test will reveal what sort of works we have done, whether good or bad. The Scripture passages in Figure 13 provide some indication of what comprises good works and bad works.

∾ ∾ ∾

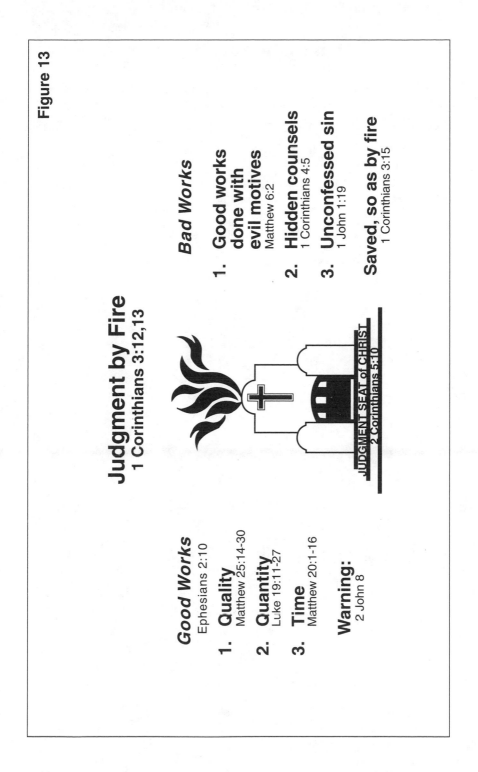

Figure 13

Don't Lose Your Rewards

Many Christians assume that earned rewards, the result of good works done since their salvation, can never be lost. Evaluate these verses with that assumption in mind:

1 Corinthians 3:14:

What if a Christian's works don't endure the test of fire?

2 John 8:

What is implied by "full reward"?

Revelation 3:11 suggests what?

What should you conclude from these three verses?

If earned rewards can be lost or subtracted from, what could cause their loss? (Consider, for example, the condition on which 1 John 1:9 is based.)

What if a person does not confess his sin?

What could cause loss, based on 1 Corinthians 4:5?

When Good Works Turn to Stubble

Read Matthew 6:2 and explain why some good works will receive no reward.

Ephesians 6:7 tells to whom service should be rendered:

Colossians 3:17 tells who should be glorified by what we do:

Colossians 3:23 makes it clear how good works should be done:

Do you think some church work is done with wrong motives? Give some examples.

Based on these Scriptures and 1 Corinthians 3:14,15, do you think some believers might be in for a surprise when they are judged for their works?

≈ ≈ ≈

Summary

Because our Lord challenged us to "lay up for yourselves treasure in heaven, where neither moth nor rust destroys and where thieves do not break in and steal" (Matthew 6:20), many Christians think that earned rewards are forever secure. What they do not realize is that although no other person or power can take these rewards from us, we can destroy them ourselves by the way we live.

I'm sure you are aware of certain well-known Christians who have served the Lord faithfully for many years but then through a moral indiscretion or some other sin brought reproach to the cause of Christ. The judgment seat of Christ will reveal all truth, even unconfessed failure and sin. The works judged in 1 Corinthians 3:12-15 evidently all looked alike until after the fire tested every man's work. There would be no purpose in using fire to test straw or wood or stubble—unless they looked the same as gold, silver, or jewels. It is the holy test of fire that will determine whether our works were good or bad. To the church, a person's "Christian service" may look like good works, but any motives will be revealed by Christ at this judgment, and this person may lose his or her reward on account of self-seeking motives or hypocrisy.

Some of the verses we looked at in the previous study guide showed that a Christian can lose his crown, receive less than a full reward, and "suffer loss" even when expecting rewards. There are at least three things that could cause a loss of reward: unconfessed sin, good things done with an evil motive, and hidden counsels of the heart that are displeasing to God.

How all this will turn out is known only to God. What's important is the fact that God's work should be done in God's way—with a pure heart and a desire to glorify Him—or else there will be no reward, or, at best, a diminished reward. Also, God is not interested in having us serve Him faithfully for just a few years, but rather for our entire lifetime. Paul challenges us with this exhortation at the end of the great resurrection chapter we've already studied: "Therefore, my beloved brethren, be steadfast, immovable, always abounding in the work of the Lord, knowing that your labor is not in vain in the Lord" (1 Corinthians 15:58).

For those whose faithful service provides them with genuine rewards that survive the fire test, Scripture promises crowns. Since the Bible tells us that we will reign with Christ (2 Timothy 2:12) in His kingdom, it is obvious what these crowns signify, for crowns are for rulers. That is compatible with Jesus' parable of the pounds, in which He promised to give rewards according to a person's service when He taught that the person who was faithful with ten pounds would be made a ruler over ten cities.

That may be the reason the judgment seat of Christ occurs just prior to the millennial kingdom—so that Christians can be assigned to opportunities of service according to the faithful use of their talents in directly or indirectly advancing Christ's spiritual kingdom in this life. What's more, special insight can be gained by examining the different types of crowns mentioned in Scripture.

~ ~ ~

The Five Crowns for Service

Read the following Bible verses and tell, as best you can, what kind of crown is mentioned and how it is earned. Then compare your answer with the summary that appears afterward.

2 Timothy 4:8

1 Corinthians 9:25-27

What is the difference between those two crowns?

James 1:12; Revelation 2:10

1 Thessalonians 2:19

1 Peter 5:4

Who wears crowns in this life?

Who will wear them in the next life?

~ ~ ~

Summary

We have already seen that a crown is a symbol of rulership and that these crowns are given on the basis of faithful service. The apostle Paul challenged Timothy, "Make full proof of thy ministry" (2 Timothy 4:5). In other words, we are to take advantage of all opportunities to use our talents to the maximum to advance God's kingdom while we are alive on this earth. Any faithful Christian can earn at least one of these crowns, and many will earn several.

The Crown of Righteousness

The reason many Christians are not used by God is because they do not live a righteous life. It is not easy to live a righteous life in an unrighteous age; it is a constant fight. But the eternal reward will be well worth it. Second Timothy 4:8 suggests that if we live in the attitude that our Lord could come soon, we will be driven to live the kind of life He will approve of: "There is laid up for me the crown of righteousness, which the Lord, the righteous Judge, will give to me on that Day, and not to me only but also to all who have loved His appearing."

The Incorruptible Crown

This "imperishable crown" mentioned in 1 Corinthians 9:25-27 is often called "the victor's crown." It is different from the crown of righteousness; this is the crown that is given to the faithful servant who denies himself and his personal desires in order to win the race in faithful service. He doesn't just avoid sin; in order to better serve his Lord, he avoids even some good things that other Christians enjoy.

Paul used runners as an illustration. They deny themselves personal time and relaxation to arduously train their body in order to win their race. Some Christians deny themselves financially to serve the Lord. I have often thought of teachers at Christian schools who scrimp on a tight budget because their salary is 25 to 50 percent lower than they would receive by teaching in the public sector. Many missionaries have to deny themselves years of family contact to bring the gospel to places far from home, and the list goes on. This crown seems to be a reward for self-denial—a crown that few Christians in this self-indulgent age will receive.

Moses is a good example of a believer who will probably be given such a crown. While he could have remained as the number-two man in Egypt, Scripture tells us:

> By faith Moses, when he became of age, refused to be called the son of Pharaoh's daughter, choosing rather to suffer affliction with the people of God than to enjoy the passing pleasures of sin, esteeming

the reproach of Christ greater riches than the treasures in Egypt; for he looked to the reward (Hebrews 11:24-26).

The Crown of Life

James 1:12 and Revelation 2:10 indicate that there is a special crown for those Christians who are persecuted for righteousness' sake. It is sometimes called "the martyr's crown," for it goes to those who have been cruelly killed because of their testimony and service for the Master.

God, in His sovereignty, has chosen to allow the martyrdom or persecution of some Christians during this church age, when He expects people to call on Him by faith in the teaching of His Word rather than by miracles and signs (such as were practiced during the first century, before the Bible was completed). While it seems unfair to us when fellow believers are unjustly persecuted, we can be sure of this: All martyrs will be adequately compensated in the life to come.

The Crown of Rejoicing

First Thessalonians 2:19 indicates that there is a special soul-winner's crown for those individuals who have majored in leading people to faith in Christ. Paul was such an individual. The people to whom he spoke were his "crown of rejoicing" because he had led them to Christ and taught them in the faith. Note that this is called the "crown of rejoicing"—keep in mind that the angels in heaven rejoice when a sinner comes to faith (Luke 15:7). In the light of eternity, soul-winning is the most important thing in the world. All our busy activity and the "things" of this earth pale into insignificance in the light of eternity, for in that day the things of the world will be burned up and forgotten, and only what's done for Christ will last.

Almost every church has faithful individuals whose greatest joy is leading people to Christ. They are a minority; they are the ones who faithfully come out on "visitation night" to share their faith. They witness to those with whom they work, and they pray for God

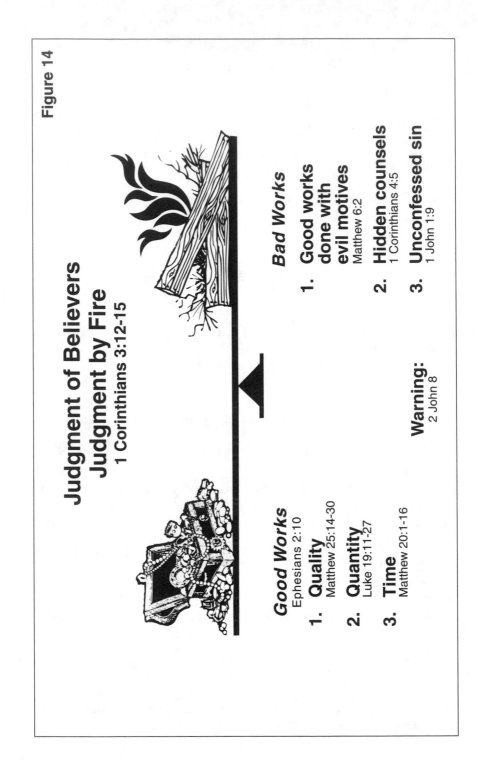

Figure 14

to use them in sharing the gospel. My mother, who went to be with the Lord a few years ago, was like that. In fact, when I visited her one week before she died, she asked me to pray for two things: "That the Lord will call me home soon, and that He will use me to lead one more soul to Him before I go." She had her chance three days before she died. While serving as a crisis pregnancy hotline counselor (which she often did), a 17-year-old pregnant girl called in desperation for help. She was phone-patched to my mother's home, where, after an hour's conversation, she prayed to receive Christ. Not a bad legacy for my mother to leave her children and grandchildren!

The Crown of Glory

First Peter 5:1,4 tells us about the "elder's crown," or as Peter calls it, "the crown of glory." There seems to be a special crown for those spiritual elders who share the Word of God. They could be ministers, Sunday school teachers, child evangelism teachers, or anyone who teaches the Word of God faithfully to others. Such individuals rarely get adequate rewards in this life, but they certainly will be rewarded in the life to come.

Now that we have examined these five crowns, it would be good to take a few minutes to analyze which of these crowns you may receive. Don't live such a self-centered, unsurrendered life that you have no crown at all on judgment day. Remember, we are in a race—a long one. Some Christians make good sprinters and serve the Lord well for a few years, but it is a wise servant who always keeps his body under discipline, lives a holy life year after year, wins as many people to Christ as he can, endures persecution when necessary, and teaches the Word of God whenever possible. Such a Christian will not regret this kind of life on judgment day!

The judgment seat of Christ will be an exciting experience for the faithful child of God—which I hope you are. But it will be a miserable "judgment of loss" for those who love the world and the things of this world so much that they never get around to serving the Lord, who paid an enormous price to save them.

Figure 14 describes their plight:

> If anyone's work which he has built on it endures, he will receive a reward. If anyone's work is burned, he will suffer loss; but he himself will be saved, yet so as through fire (1 Corinthians 3:14,15).

The purpose of the judgment seat of Christ is to reward faithful servants with job assignments for the millennial kingdom. You will serve Christ during that period in direct proportion to the way you have faithfully served Him during this time on earth. If you have been a spectator Christian in this life, you will be one in the next. Your reward earned from this life will determine what kind of opportunity you have to serve Christ for 1,000 years. In the final analysis, it is entirely up to you how you will spend those 1,000 years!

The second advent, as it is often called today, refers to that "day of the Lord" when Christ shall come again to this earth in power and great glory to rule and reign personally over this earth. As we have seen, most of the many biblical references to the second coming refer to the glorious appearing when Christ will come as King of kings and Lord of lords, fulfilling the portion of Isaiah 9:6,7 that says "the government will be upon His shoulder...[and] of the increase of His government and peace there will be no end."

Our Lord will be the last world emperor and His rule will extend into eternity. However, as we shall see, His kingdom will be unlike any that ever existed before. It will be a kingdom of peace and prosperity, the curse on the earth will be lifted, and man's inhumanity to man will cease. For the first time since the Garden of Eden, man will love his neighbor as himself.

But before Christ sets up His kingdom, He must come in power and great glory. Let's learn more about that in this next study guide.

~ ~ ~

The Glorious Appearing
Revelation 19

Go back to pages 42-43 and restudy the passages that describe this event. In one sentence, write a summary of those texts.

What precedes the second coming, according to Revelation 19:5-9?

Read Revelation 19:11-21 and write down the five titles used for the Lord Jesus Christ.

1)

2)

3)

4)

5)

Who is the rider on the white horse in verse 11?

What is his weapon of war (verse 15)?

How does he slay the multitudes (verse 21)?

What happens to the kings of the earth (verses 19-21)?

What happens to the beast (verse 20)?

What happens to the False Prophet (verse 20)?

What happens to Satan (Revelation 20:1-3)?

≈ ≈ ≈

Summary

The next time Christ comes to earth, it will not be to suffer, as He did in His first coming. This time He will come in power and great glory on a white horse, accompanied by the angelic hosts of heaven and His Bride, the church, which He has just purified and judged in preparation for ruling this earth.

All those who hate God will be gathered together against Christ to do war with Him. They will be led by the Antichrist or the beast, who is indwelt by Satan himself. With him will be the False Prophet and the Christ-rejecting kings of the earth. They will bring the largest armies of the world ever gathered in what the Bible calls "the battle of that great day of God Almighty," popularly called the Battle of Armageddon.

But this will be one war where there is no fighting! The combatants will be prepared to fight, but our Lord's awesome power will consume them in one moment by the word of His mouth—and all those who accepted the mark of the beast during the Tribulation will be consumed. This will conclude the seven-year Tribulation period and usher in the kingdom over which Christ will reign. At this time Christ will judge the nations and decide who can enter the millennial kingdom.

≈ ≈ ≈

The Judgment of the Nations
Matthew 25:31-46

When does this event occur (verse 31)?

Who stands before Christ (verse 32a)?

How will He separate the people (verses 32,33)?

What is the basis on which He makes this separation (verses 34-40)?

Why do some miss the kingdom (verses 41-46)?

What will happen to these people (verse 46)?

Do people enter Christ's kingdom by faith or by works?

How do you relate this to Ephesians 2:8,9?

≈ ≈ ≈

Summary

When Christ returns at the end of the Tribulation and finishes His glorious appearing, there will be only two kinds of people left on the earth: 1) the Jews, and 2) those who are good to the Jews (whom Jesus called "My brethren" in Matthew 25:40). This latter group will be among those who refuse to follow the Antichrist by worshiping him and taking his mark. Instead, they will risk their lives by endeavoring to protect the Jews, who are targeted for persecution by the Antichrist. All those who accept the mark of the beast during the Tribulation period will be killed at Christ's coming. Those who had accepted the mark of the heavenly Father will be martyred during the seven-year tribulation; they are the Tribulation saints described in Revelation 7.

The purpose of the judgment of the nations is to determine who enters Christ's kingdom in their natural bodies. In all likelihood it will not be a huge population. It will consist of only two kinds of natural-bodied people—converted Israel and those Gentile believers who, during the Tribulation, defied the Antichrist and reached out to help the Jews and others in time of need.

During this time, God will fulfill the many Old Testament prophecies given to the nation of Israel. He will "create a new heart in them" to obey His will and commit themselves to a lifetime of serving Him. With Satan bound so he cannot tempt the world, the kingdom age, with its Edenic or Utopian existence, will be unlike any period the world has ever known.

There's one important fact we should observe while we are on this subject: The church will not usher in the kingdom by taking over the governments of the world. The Tribulation will end with only a few believers on the earth. The Antichrist will be in control, and the earth will be filled with leaders who hate God and His followers. This is why it is necessary for Christ to come in great power and glory and wrest control of the world from these evil forces. He will then judge the nations by separating the sheep from the goats (Matthew 25:31-46). The sheep are believers who go into the kingdom, and the goats will be cast into "everlasting fire" (verse 41).

Why the Rapture Cannot Be Posttribulational

Before leaving this discussion about the population of the millennium, we need to recognize that one reason we know posttribulationism (the belief that Christ will rapture the church at the end of the Tribulation) cannot be true is that there would be no one left on earth to enter the millennial kingdom. Remember, the unsaved goats on Christ's left will be cast into hell. If those who remain are raptured at the end of the Tribulation, there would be no one on earth to produce the enormous population the Bible says will exist during the millennium.

Since we know that redeemed Israel and all other believers who survive the Tribulation will enter the millennium in their natural bodies and they will be the individuals who populate the 1,000-year kingdom, we can know that a posttribulation rapture is simply not possible.

Various Views of the Kingdom

During the 2,000-year history of the church there have been three primary views of our Lord's return in relation to the millennial kingdom. These views are called *premillennialism, postmillennialism,* and *amillennialism.*

Premillennialism. This is the oldest of the views and dominated the thinking of the early Christians for the first three centuries. Basically the prefix *pre* means that Christ will come again *before* the kingdom or 1,000-year millennium. This is the view held in this book.

Amillennialism. A indicates "no," meaning that no literal millennium is expected by those who hold this view. They believe that the spiritual kingdom of Christ has operated simultaneously with the earthly satanic kingdom for 2,000 years, and that there will be only one general resurrection (when Christ will separate the saved and lost), followed by heaven. This view was popularized by Augustine in the fourth century, and it became the dominant view of Roman Catholicism (and still is to this day). During the Dark Ages, when Christians had little access to the Bible, this view went almost unchallenged. But after the Bible was translated and printed in the fifteenth century so that Christians could study it for themselves, Protestantism emerged, which emphasized many Bible doctrines long forgotten, such as justification by faith. Eventually, such Bible study also revived premillennialism.

Postmillennialism. This view holds that Christ will come *after* the earthly kingdom. Proponents believe that we are in (or entering) the kingdom already, that the church is gaining ground on the earth, and that it will become so strong that it will governmentally

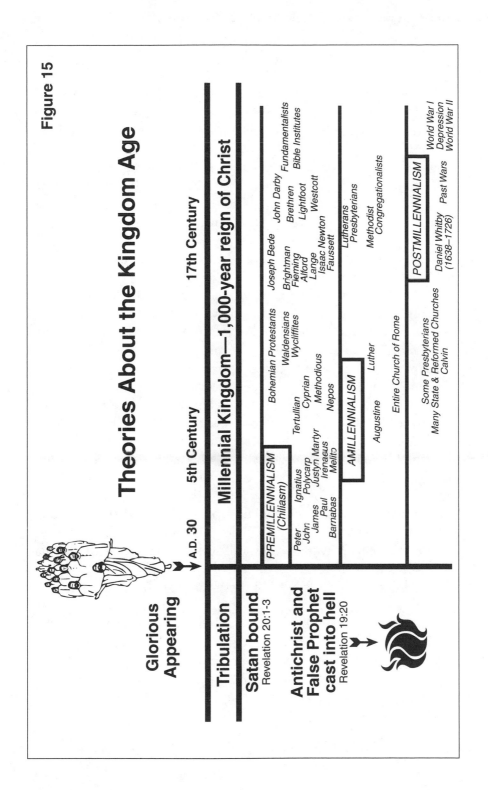

Figure 15

usher in the era of peace described in prophecy—after which Christ will return.

This view was popularized by the writings of Daniel Whitby (1638–1726), who was a Unitarian, a liberal, and a freethinker. The theory dovetailed with the evolutionary view of man and the initiation of the industrial revolution. For a while, the future appeared bright. People looked for a Utopian state on earth, a golden age of converted people brought about by the noble efforts of the church, after which Christ would return. However, Whitby's writings on the Godhead were publicly burned and he was denounced as a heretic. Yet his millennial view was keyed to the times, for it expressed what people wanted to hear and initiated a prophetic school of considerable influence.*

Postmillennialism, with its Utopian view of the future, fell on hard times during this century, following two world wars and the unmatched inhumanities of Communism inspired by both the Soviets and Chinese. In addition, because postmillennialism allegorizes prophecy, this view has not had much acceptance among Bible-believing Christians. In recent years reconstructionists and dominionists have tried to revive it, but it has made few inroads among those who take a literal view of prophecy. For example, Revelation 20, which six times in six verses indicates that the length of the kingdom age will be 1,000 years, must be taken either literally or figuratively. If you take those statements literally, you are probably a premillennialist. If you take them symbolically, you are probably either a postmillennialist or amillennialist. There are, however, some fine Christians who take the Bible literally (yet interpret prophecy symbolically, although it is my belief that doing so creates more problems than it solves. Figure 15 on page 165 should be studied in the light of these three views).

Premillennialism, which has been under a small but noisy attack today by some of the above-mentioned postmillennialists, traces its roots back to the apostles Paul (2 Thessalonians 2:1-12) and John (Revelation) as well as most of the early church fathers. This view dropped out of sight during the Dark Ages (dark because the Bible was kept in monasteries and museums and not accessible to the common people).

---

* Adapted from Gerald B. Stanton, *Why I Am a Premillennialist* (private publication, 1976), p. 4.

Later, as Bibles began to be printed and distributed and Christians began studying God's Word for themselves, premillennialism came back on the scene. It was widely popularized by John Darby, the founder of the Brethren movement, a church deeply committed to Bible study during the middle of the nineteenth century. In the twentieth century, premillennialism became the dominant view of the Bible-believing church through the writings of C.I. Scofield (author of the Scofield Bible notes) as well as through the Fundamentalist movement of the 1920s and 1930s and the teachings of Dallas Theological Seminary (and certain other schools). Almost all Bible institutions and Christian colleges that did *not* come from a reformed or covenant church background hold to a premillennial perspective. Such institutions and colleges were committed to taking the Bible literally rather than imposing a certain end-times position onto the Scriptures to arrive at a particular interpretation of the Scriptures. If you take the Bible literally, then you will come to the conclusion that Jesus Christ will someday come back to this earth and set up His kindom, and it will last, according to Revelation 20, for 1,000 years.

Premillennialism does not answer every complex question of prophecy, but for those who endeavor to interpret the Scriptures literally, it answers far more questions than any other view of prophecy.

15

THE COMING KINGDOM
OF CHRIST

Both Jews and Christians agree that someday their Messiah is going to come to set up His kingdom and rule on this earth. It will be a time of peace, blessing, and joy that will be interrupted only briefly at the end, before eternity or heaven is ushered in. There is, of course, great disagreement on the identity of that Messiah. Christians believe that Jesus Christ is that Messiah, and that He will return to set up His kingdom and that they will rule it with Him. Jews, on the other hand, believe that a not-yet-known Jew will yet come as Messiah to set up that kingdom. What is interesting is that most Jews are unaware that the requirements of their Messiah make Him identical to Jesus Christ! But both groups agree that when Messiah comes, He will reign over this earth.

There are far too many passages in the Bible that predict a future kingdom than we could possibly study in this book. We can, however, select some of the most significant passages. Again, rather than prejudice you to accept my position before you formulate your own, I will suggest some select passages for you to study so you can come to your own conclusions. Then, in the summary, I will give my commentary. I trust you'll find this a most interesting and inspiring study!

≈ ≈ ≈

The Coming Kingdom

Isaiah 9:6,7 is one of several passages that merge the first and second comings of Christ into one prophecy. What do these verses teach about His first coming?

Were you surprised to find that most of this passage relates to the second coming?

Who will bear the weight of the government (verse 6a)?

Write the five titles ascribed to Christ in verse 6.

   1)

   2)

   3)

   4)

   5)

Describe how His kingdom will flourish (verse 7).

What is meant by the term "throne of David"?

How long will this kingdom last?

List three words that describe Christ's kingdom.

    1)

    2)

    3)

Who guarantees this kingdom (verse 7c)?

≈ ≈ ≈

The Future Kingdom in the Old Testament

Daniel 2:31-35 contains a most important prophecy given by God to a pagan king, a man who may have been the most absolute ruler in the history of the world. Read this passage and explain it in your own words.

Daniel 2:37-45 gives God's interpretation of the aformentioned vision (through Daniel). Study it carefully and describe it.

Who sets up the "rock" kingdom?

Who is the "rock"?

Isaiah 61:1-11 is the passage our Lord quoted while in the synagogue at Nazareth. We saw how He claimed that His first coming fulfilled verses 1 through 2a (Luke 4:21). Study all 11 verses, and list briefly seven characteristics of the future kingdom.

    1)

    2)

    3)

    4)

5)

6)

7)

By any stretch of the imagination, could this ever have occurred in past history?

≈ ≈ ≈

Conditions of the Future Kingdom
Isaiah 65:13-25

List five things mentioned in Isaiah 65:19-23 that will not exist in Christ's glorious kingdom.

1)

2)

3)

4)

5)

How old are the children in this kingdom (verse 20b)?

Who dies at that age (verse 20c)?

How permanent and prosperous will the kingdom be (verses 21-23)?

What does verse 24 suggest?

Write about the conditions mentioned in verse 25.

~ ~ ~

The Two Phases of the Kingdom in the New Testament

There are almost 200 references to the kingdom in the New Testament, but unlike the Old Testament, most of them (except for those in the book of Revelation) have to do with the *spiritual* phase of the kingdom. To save you confusion, allow me to explain these two phases of the kingdom.

The *spiritual* phase of the kingdom is what our Lord came to establish in His first coming. He told Pontius Pilate that He was a King, but that His kingdom "is not of this world" (John 18:36). He also said that a person must be "born again" to get into His kingdom (John 3:3). John the Baptist said that people had to "repent" to get into the kingdom of God (Matthew 3:1). We have already studied Paul's assertion that "flesh and blood cannot inherit the kingdom of God" (1 Corinthians 15:50). So the Lord first of all established a *spiritual* kingdom into which people are born by faith in Christ's death, burial, and resurrection. Such individuals are then entitled to enter the *literal* kingdom of God on this earth when Christ comes physically to set it up.

That is why any attempt to establish the kingdom of God on earth before Christ comes is doomed to failure. The task of the church today is not "kingdom building." Instead, it is to advance the spiritual kingdom by preaching the gospel around the world. This does not mean that Christians who are members of that spiritual kingdom by faith in Christ do not have a responsibility to be both salt and light during this present age (see Matthew 5:13,14). Christians are to be salt in that they are a morally savoring influence on society by participating as good citizens in voting, running for office, and serving both their God and their country as good stewards.

Some do this as schoolteachers, ministers, attorneys, authors, artists, or movie producers, and others by running for public office as school board members, city councilmen, congressmen, senators, and so on. All responsible "salty citizens" will be careful to vote on election day to keep anti-Christians from ruling over us and limiting our freedom to fulfill our primary task, which is to be the light of the world in fulfillment of the Great Commission. Hopefully, in the closing years of the church age, Christians will be more faithful in these dual challenges than was Israel in the Old Testament.

The kingdom our Lord will set up when He comes will be made up of three groups of people: 1) Jews who survive the Tribulation and accept Christ as their Messiah (and who still have their natural bodies); 2) Gentile believers who were good to the Jews (also alive in their natural bodies); and 3) the resurrected saints of all ages (who will have their resurrected bodies).

Except for Revelation 20, most of the New Testament passages on the kingdom have to do with the spiritual phase of the kingdom, which is often mentioned interchangeably with the church. Examine, for example, Matthew 16:16-19, where our Lord told Peter He would "build My church" on the rock of Peter's testimony that Christ was "the Son of the living God." He then promised to give Peter "the keys of the kingdom of heaven" ("the kingdom of God" and "the kingdom of heaven" are often used interchangeably—compare Matthew 13 and Mark 4). "the kingdom of God" in the New Testament usually refers to the true church, that body of believers who enter the church by faith in Christ and then spend the rest of their lives sharing that faith so others can also become members of the church. The literal physical kingdom is yet future and is best described in the Old Testament and Revelation 20. It will be set up when Christ returns in power, because He alone has the power to set it up.

≈ ≈ ≈

Conditions During Christ's Kingdom

What happens to Satan at the beginning of Christ's kingdom (Revelation 20:1-3)?

What effect will that have on the earth?

Why is Satan bound during the millennial kingdom (verse 3b)?

What effect will that have on faith and people coming to Christ?

Who will enter this kingdom, according to verse 4?

What will those people do during the millennial kingdom, and for how long?

How many times is the duration of the kingdom mentioned in verses 2-7?

Why is that important?

What does verse 6 say the resurrected saints will do during the kingdom?

Why is Satan released at the end of the millennial kingdom (verses 7,8)?

How successful will Satan be (verses 8,9)?

Then what happens to Satan (verse 10)?

Who is already there?

What does that suggest about the length of time for eternal suffering?

According to verse 10, how long will those who are in the lake of fire suffer?

Then what will happen (verses 11-15)?

≈ ≈ ≈

A Wondrous Age

Ever since the fall of Adam and Eve in the Garden of Eden, humanity and creation have been under the judgment and ramifications of their original sin. The pollution of sin has affected all of humanity and all of creation. The apostle Paul reminds us of that which we experience daily when he declares in Romans 8:22, "We know that the whole creation has been groaning as in the pains of childbirth right up to the present time" (NIV). However, during the 1,000-year millennial kingdom there will be a partial lifting of the curse and ramifications of original sin. There will still be death (for those who entered the millennium in their natural bodies), and the complete effects of the Fall will not be lifted until the creation of the new heaven and new earth in the eternal state after the millennium (Revelation 22:3).

The coming literal kingdom of Christ to this earth will be the most blessed time this world has known since the Garden of Eden. In fact, many Edenic features will characterize it. All those who rebelled against God will be gone. Satan will be bound literally so he cannot tempt man, and Christ will enforce righteousness. Of course, this righteousness will be enforced with the help of His holy angels and the church. No doubt it will be illegal for pornographers, criminals, and others who traditionally corrupt society to ply their evil trades.

The coming kingdom will be a time of unprecedented prosperity, when everyone will have his own home. The curse on the earth will be lifted and the ground will bear incredible harvests. Cheating and war will be nonexistent, so people will be able to enjoy the fruits of their labors.

Isaiah 65 indicates that longevity will be increased to almost what it was prior to the flood, when people lived to almost 1000 years of age. At least that will be the case for believers, who will live from the time of their birth until the end of the kingdom. Isaiah 65:20 indicates that a person will be considered still a child at 100 years of age.

Not only will lifespans be considerably longer in the millennial kingdom, but the world population will be enormous. Jeremiah 33:22 speaks of this large population: "As the host of heaven cannot be numbered, nor the sand of the sea measured, so will I multiply the descendants of David My servant and the Levites who minister to me." In Zechariah 8:5 we read that "the streets of the city shall be full of boys and girls," proving that the population in Israel will increase dramatically. Keep in mind that we will live under ideal conditions in the millennial kingdom—there will be no wars to wipe out large numbers of people, and there will be no abortion to murder massive numbers of babies.

A Time of Faith

The millennial kingdom will be a time of faith, when the majority of the population will become believers. We see that in several Bible passages. Christ will be in charge, so there won't be immoral or other forms of destructive TV programming available to blind men's minds to the gospel. Body-damaging substances will not be available, so people will not have their minds so fogged that they cannot fairly appraise the truths of Scripture; Satan will be bound so he cannot "blind their eyes." The university chairs of learning will not be dominated by atheists set on turning the minds of young people away from God. Instead, all education will start from the premise "In the beginning GOD!" In such an academic climate, young people will be more open than ever to the claims of God and Christ on their lives. Even art forms will glorify Christ during the millennial kingdom. Jeremiah 31:31-34 indicates that everyone will be so acquainted with the gospel that no one will need to share it with his neighbor.

Isaiah 65:20 indicates that unbelievers will die "being 100 years old." That suggests enormous consequences for the high percentage of believers living at that time, for it indicates that only Christians will live beyond their hundredth birthday. Evidently God will give people 100 years to decide about Christ. If they accept Him, they are permitted to live on for the rest of the kingdom period. But no sinner will survive his hundredth birthday. That fact alone would mean that only Christians will be alive to propagate and raise children after they are 100 years old. Based on this fact, along with the ideal cultural environment present during this era, it is possible that as high as 80 or more percent of the population will be saved during that age.

The government and politics of the millennial kingdom will focus on the benevolent reign of Jesus Christ as Israel's Messiah-King. It will be a theocracy centered in Jerusalem (Isaiah 2:1-4), where Jesus will reign as both Messiah and King of Israel, thus fulfilling God's prophetic promise to King David in the Davidic Covenant (2 Samuel 7:12-16). God's covenant with David guaranteed David's dynasty, throne, and kingdom would continue forever. When Jesus Christ returns at the end of the Tribulation, He will reestablish the Davidic throne in His personal rule (Jeremiah 23:5-8). Other significant passages describing Christ's reign over Israel include Psalm 2, Isaiah 9:6,7, Jeremiah 33:20-26, Ezekiel 34:23-25 and 37:23,24, and Luke 1:32,33. These and other Bible passages provide ample specific evidence that the kingdom promised to David will be fully realized in the future.

A Rebellious Youth Movement

But in spite of all the ideal conditions arranged by God to attract a maximum number of people to accept His free gift of salvation by receiving His Son, many will rebel at the end of the 1,000-year kingdom, for Revelation 20 indicates that at the end of the 1,000 years Satan will be loosed from the bottomless pit to go out "to deceive the nations"—that is, to tempt them to rebel against God. The reason God allows this to happen is so that all the unsaved people living on the earth will be forced to make a decision about whether they will receive Christ before God establishes the eternal order. We have already seen that these unsaved will be people under 100 years of age, according to Isaiah 65:20, for only believers will live past their hundredth birthday.

What's sad is that even after living for almost 100 years under the righteous reign of Christ, there will still be a multitude "whose number is as the sand of the sea" (Revelation 20:8) who will rebel against God when given the opportunity. Among other things, this suggests that it isn't entirely Satan's fault that people reject faith in Christ, but rather, people rebel by their own will. Satan's appearance on the scene at this point will simply bring to the surface the rebellion within the hearts of those who "are not willing to come" to Him that they might have eternal life (John 5:40).

The End of Satan

Revelation 20:10 says, "And the devil, who deceived them, was cast into the lake of fire and brimstone where the beast and the false prophet are. And they will be tormented day and night forever and ever." The ability of living creatures to suffer indefinitely in the lake of fire is seen in the fact that the beast (or Antichrist) and the False Prophet are men. They are thrown into the lake of fire at the beginning of the 1,000-year kingdom (Revelation 19:20), yet they are spoken of in the present tense in Revelation 20:10, indicating that they are still there. It is into this lake of fire that Satan will be cast. He, the Antichrist, the False Prophet, and all those from every age in history who rejected God's free offer of salvation through faith in Christ "be tormented day and night forever and ever." The Bible clearly states, then, that this punishment will last for all eternity!

The Two Stages of the First Resurrection

The Bible is a book of life—eternal life. Yet we are faced every day with the reality of death, from the deaths of babies to the deaths of elderly people. The only way to correlate these two contrasting states of life and death is to remember that *all the dead will eventually be resurrected.* We have already seen that our Lord's bodily resurrection guarantees the Christian's eventual resurrection.

It is important to realize that there are *two* resurrections in Scripture: 1) "the first resurrection" (also called "the resurrection unto life") and 2) "the second resurrection" (which is the same as "the resurrection of damnation," or judgment). Daniel, the great Old Testament prophet, associated both of these resurrections with the time of the end, when "there shall be a time of trouble, such as never was since there was a nation...." Then he added, "Many of those who sleep in the dust of the earth shall awake, some to everlasting life, some to shame and everlasting contempt" (Daniel 12:1,2).

The first resurrection is not a single event, but takes place in two stages that are separated by at least seven years.

The first stage of the first resurrection is the rapture of the church, which, as we have already seen, includes both living and dead Christians. When the Lord shouts for His church from heaven,

He will resurrect the dead in Christ (all those who "sleep in Jesus"). Then "we who are alive and remain shall be caught up together with them in the clouds to meet the Lord in the air. And thus we shall always be with the Lord" (1 Thessalonians 4:17). Very simply, this means that all those who have received Jesus Christ as their personal Savior, whether living or dead at the time He comes in the air to rapture His church, will be a part of this first stage of the first resurrection. The most comforting aspect of this resurrection is the promise that no matter what happens after that, we will "always be with the Lord."

What many people don't seem to realize is that the first resurrection has *two stages*. After the first stage, millions of people will yet call upon the name of the Lord and be saved, principally during the seven-year Tribulation. Then, when our Lord comes to this earth to set up His 1,000-year kingdom of righteousness, He will resurrect the remaining believers. In the words of the prophet John:

> And I saw thrones, and they [the saints] sat on them, and judgment was committed to them. And I saw the souls of those who had been beheaded for their witness to Jesus and for the word of God, who had not worshiped the beast or his image, and had not received his mark on their foreheads or on their hands. And they lived and reigned with Christ for a thousand years (Revelation 20:4).

Then he writes:

> But the rest of the dead [the unbelievers] did not live again until the thousand years were finished. This is the first resurrection. Blessed and holy is he who has part in the first resurrection. Over such the second death [eternal condemnation] has no power, but they shall be priests of God and of Christ, and shall reign with Him a thousand years (Revelation 20:5,6).

The second stage of the first resurrection will probably include (according to Psalm 50:1-6) all the Old Testament saints who went to their graves with faith in God and His future sacrifice for their sin, as well as all the Tribulation saints, most of whom will have been martyred because they refused to worship the Antichrist. These shall "be priests," and, like Christians raised at the rapture and judged for their works as believers, "they will reign with Him a thousand years."

The "rest of the dead," or all the unbelievers who lived from the days of Adam and Eve until the time Christ comes to set up His kingdom, will not be raised until the end of that kingdom age, which comes just before eternity. They will take part in what is called "the second resurrection." It is a resurrection of the lost to judgment and then to eternal separation from God. But before we can examine more about that resurrection, we must back up slightly and find out where these individuals are now.

16

WHERE THE DEAD ARE NOW

The most traumatic event in my life was my father's death; he died three weeks before my tenth birthday. Until a person has gone through the tragedy of the loss of a close loved one, he rarely thinks about death. We tend to assume that life goes on forever, but the death of a loved one destroys those illusions and raises questions that we may have never before contemplated.

In my case, the first question I asked my mother was, "Where is Dad now?" That is probably the most commonly asked question under those circumstances, and not only by children. Everyone is curious about life in the afterlife. As far back as we can go in history, man has asked Job's classic question: "If a man dies, shall he live again?" (Job 14:14). Life is so precious to human beings that the desire to live on in some future state is almost universal. Library shelves are filled with books on the subject, and practically every religion known to man offers some kind of teaching on the subject.

Looking back, I detect something interesting about my childhood reaction to my father's death that is common to many people. At no time did I consider the possibility that he had ceased to exist, for my question indicated my assurance that he, the real person, was still alive somewhere. I just didn't know where. Fortunately for me (and certainly my father), my parents had become Christians six years before he died. As I discovered later, that was the most important decision he ever made, for it determined where he spent his after-life.

Due to my boyhood experience with my father's death, I have studied the subject in great detail. My library is stocked with collections of books and articles on the subject from all over the world. And it is my opinion that no one will be accurately informed on death until he studies the Bible's teaching and interprets all other writings in the light of it.

The Bible is a book of life, not of death. Yet like any book of history, it has to include the fact that men and women die. But the Bible also points out that humans, while alive on earth, can make arrangements to enjoy eternal life in the next world. Although the Bible focuses extensively upon eternal and physical *life*, it also treats the subject of death many times. The 66 books of the Bible have much to say about death and the future life, since God meant for man to know the truth. He knew that ignorance would arouse some of man's greatest fears. Yet when an individual knows God personally and is aware of what Scripture teaches about the afterlife, he is not afraid of death.

To get a comprehensive picture of what God says about death, we must turn to several books of the Bible and consider various references in the light of others, thereby building a composite description. If you are fascinated by the subject of life in the afterlife, you will find our study most rewarding.

The World of the Dead

The 39 books of the Old Testament refer to the world of the dead 65 times as *Sheol*. The word may be translated as "the grave," "hell," or "death." Sheol must not be confused with "the pit" or "the lake of fire," for Sheol is the place of all those who have departed this life, both believers and unbelievers. The New Testament word for this world of the dead is *Hades* (appearing 42 times). It is important to note that Sheol and Hades are not really hell, as the King James version translates it. The Hebrew word *Sheol* and the Greek word *Hades* both refer to the same temporary place, whereas hell is a permanent place that lasts forever.

Tartarus, a word that occurs only once in the entire Bible (2 Peter 2:4), is defined by Bible scholars as "the deepest abyss of hades." Admittedly we don't know much about that deep abyss, except that, as part of Hades, it too is probably temporary.

Gehenna is the New Testament word for the permanent place of the dead, used by Jesus Christ Himself 11 times. James also used it (James 3:6). Of Hebrew origin from *valley* and *Hinnom*, the word refers to the Valley of Hinnom, just outside Jerusalem, where the refuse of the city was dumped. It was characteristic of this valley that a fire was continually burning there. Many Bible scholars see this as a perfect characterization of hell—a place where "the fire is not quenched" (Mark 9:48), or the "lake of fire" (Revelation 20:14), referring to the final destination of those who have rejected God.

The King James version of the Bible translates all of these words—*Sheol, Hades, Gehenna,* and *Tartarus* the same: "hell." This leads to the confusing idea that they all refer to the same place, when in fact they do not. Several modern versions of the Bible have clearly distinguished among these words. The New American Standard version, for example, calls the temporary places Sheol or Hades, and the final place of the dead "hell."

~ ~ ~

The Old Testament Teachings

Following are some of the outstanding Old Testament verses on the state of those who have died. After each Scripture reference, write what you think the verse teaches about death or the dead.

Proverbs 9:18:

Psalm 86:13:

Psalm 9:17:

Genesis 44:29:

Psalm 88:3:

Psalm 89:48:

Deuteronomy 32:22:

Song of Solomon 8:6:

Ecclesiastes 9:10:

Ezekiel 32:21:

Isaiah 14:9,10:

Psalm 49:15:

Study your answers carefully and write a synopsis of what the Old Testament teaches about life after death. Be careful not to inject anything you already know from the New Testament.

≈ ≈ ≈

The New Testament Teachings

The New Testament presumes a knowledge of the Old Testament's teachings on the afterlife. But the best teaching on this topic came from the greatest of all sources—the creator Himself, the Lord Jesus Christ.

Read Luke 16:19-31 carefully. Did Jesus call this a parable? What does that tell us?

Describe the unnamed man in verse 19, and tell what happened to him.

Describe Lazarus, and tell what happened to him.

Describe what happened to both men immediately after death (verses 22-24).

Note their contrasting lifestyles and contrasting eternities (verses 25,26).

What place separates the two states of the dead (verse 26)?

Describe the rich man's request in verses 27,28.

Why did Abraham refuse it (verse 29)?

What did the rich man recognize that his brothers needed to do in order to avoid that place (verse 30)?

How powerful a witness did Abraham think the Word of God is (verse 31)?

Study Figure 16 on the next page before reading the summary. See if you can locate the events you have just studied. Then compare your observations with the information in the summary.

≈ ≈ ≈

Summary

It is important to note that this story is not a parable, but the record of a specific experience. Characters in parables are not given

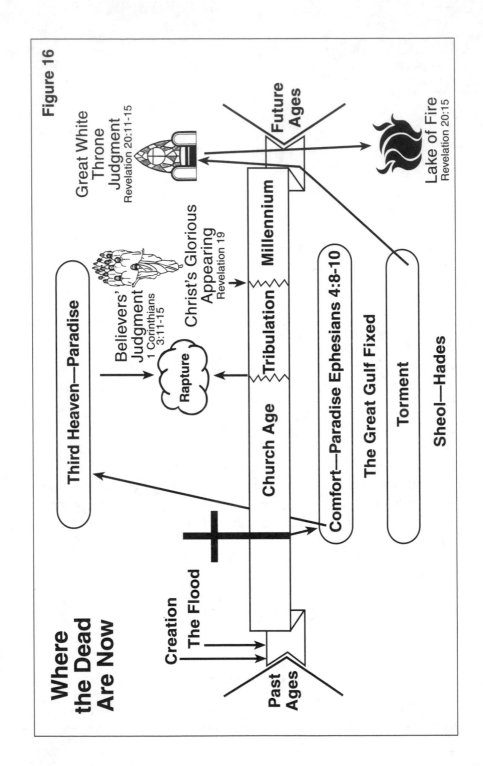

definite names but are identified as "a certain man," "a man," "a householder," and so on. This story includes names—Abraham and Lazarus—as Jesus relates the factual record of two men who lived and died (possibly just prior to the telling of the story). They both went to Hades, but not to the same part. Figure 16 (on the previous page) will clarify our Lord's teaching on this subject and will serve as a basic guide to all the future events discussed in this book.

It appears from this passage that Hades is comprised of three compartments: Abraham's bosom, the great gulf fixed, and the place of torment.

The most desirable compartment in Hades, picturesquely called Abraham's bosom or paradise, is a place of comfort. In Luke 16:25 Abraham says of Lazarus, "Now he is comforted." This would be the paradise of the Old Testament, to which the souls of the righteous dead went immediately after death. We can rightly assume that, like Lazarus, they were carried by angels to this place of comfort. It is also a place of companionship for Lazarus, since he has the joy of fellowship with Abraham. Even though he was a poor and rejected man on earth, he now holds an enviable position by the side of Abraham. This, of course, tells us of the wonderful possibility of fellowship with all the other saints of God who have gone on before: Elijah, Moses, David, and many others.

Very few details are given about the second compartment, the great gulf fixed, but we know that it is an impassable gulf over which men may look and converse but not cross. God designed it "so that those who want to pass from here to you cannot, nor can those from there pass to us" (verse 26). Evidently this is a chasm that separates the believers and unbelievers in the next life. Once a person dies, he is confined to one side or the other—comfort or torment. (Some Bible teachers also believe that this great gulf has no bottom to it, and that it could well be the bottomless pit of Revelation 20:3 into which the devil is cast at the glorious appearing of the Lord Jesus Christ.)

More details are given about the place of torment than the other compartments. The Lord Jesus was clearly interested in warning people about this place in order to keep them from going there. The rich man called Hades a *place* of torments, indicating that it is a real place and not merely a state of existence, as some people would like to believe. Luke 16:22 tells us that "the rich man also died and was buried"; verse 23 begins, "And being in torments in Hades, he lifted up his eyes." There seems to be no intermediate state; evidently a dead unbeliever goes immediately to the place of torment. Verse 23 also suggests that a person is fully conscious of what he missed, for it states that the rich man "lifted up his eyes and saw Abraham afar off, and Lazarus in his bosom." This indicates that one of the horrible tortures of Hades will be the ability of unbelievers to look across the great gulf fixed and view the comforts and blessings of believers, who are in comfort. The unbeliever will constantly be reminded of what he has missed due to his rejection of God.

It is impossible to be absolutely certain of the exact geographic location of Sheol-Hades. Some think it is in the heart of the earth, while others think it lies in some undesignated spot in the universe. The Bible refers to it as "down" in Numbers 16:33, which might be responsible for the supposition that it is in the heart of the earth. Actually, the geographic location is not important. It is crucially important, however, that this awful place of torment be avoided.

Escape from Sheol-Hades

One of the many outstanding changes brought about by the death, burial, and resurrection of Jesus Christ is that the believer does not have to go to Sheol-Hades. Psalm 16:10, as quoted by Peter in Acts 2:25-28, establishes the fact that Jesus Christ is not in Sheol-Hades today. The location of Hades is spoken of as "down," but we find in Acts 1:9,10 that the Lord Jesus was "taken up, and a cloud received Him out of [the disciples'] sight. And...they looked steadfastly toward heaven as He went up...." Second Corinthians 5:8 tells us, "We are confident, yes, well pleased rather to be absent from the body and to be present with the Lord." In other words, the believer at death does not go to Sheol-Hades, but is present with the Lord, who is not in Sheol-Hades because He dwells in heaven. In fact, the Scriptures teach that the Lord Jesus is presently "standing at the right hand of God" (Acts 7:55). Consequently, when a present-day believer (or any Christian during the church age) dies, he does not go to Sheol-Hades, but his soul proceeds immediately to heaven to be with his Savior, Jesus Christ.

One question naturally confronts us: When did this change take place? We know that the Lord Jesus went to paradise, for in Luke 23:43 He told the repentant thief on the cross, "Today you will be with Me in Paradise." So we know that Jesus went directly from the cross into the paradise section of Sheol-Hades. Now look at Ephesians 4:8-10. This passage reveals that Paradise is no longer located in Hades, but was taken by Christ up into heaven. This would indicate that a dead believer now goes to heaven, where he is joined with the Old and New Testament departed saints, leaving the former paradise section of Hades an empty compartment. It is also very possible that at this time the Lord Jesus snatched the keys of Hades and death from the hand of Satan, for we see in Revelation 1:18 that He now holds them.

You are probably wondering why the Old Testament saints were sent to the place of comfort or Paradise when they died. Why couldn't Daniel, David, Abraham, and all those great men and women of God go directly to heaven? After all, they believed in God while they lived. The answer is found in the inadequacy of the covering of their sins. In the Old Testament, sins were temporarily covered by the blood of a lamb without blemish or without spot. But an animal's blood was not sufficient to permanently cleanse their sins (Hebrews 9:9,10). Sacrifice was an exercise of obedience, in which a person showed his faith that God would someday provide permanent cleansing from sin through the perfect sacrifice of His Son.

When our Lord cried from the cross, "It is finished," He meant that the debt incurred for man's sin was paid in full. God in human flesh could accomplish what no animal sacrifice could ever do— atone for the sins of the whole world. After releasing His soul, Jesus descended into Hades and led all the Old Testament believers, who had been held captive up until the time sin was finally atoned for, up into heaven, where they are presently with Him.

The Soulish State

We need to be careful not to confuse the present conscious state of the dead with the future resurrected state of the dead. The latter is described by Paul in 1 Corinthians 15, where he speaks of the rapture at which "we shall all be changed" (verse 51). Verses 52 and 53 tell us that at the last trumpet the dead "will be raised incorruptible, and we shall be changed. For this corruptible must put on incorruption, and this mortal must put on immortality." So far, the believer has not yet received his incorruptible resurrected body. That body will be described in detail in the next chapter, but for now, remember that it is distinctly different from the present *temporary* state of the dead.

The best term I know to describe this state is "soulish." (Some call it a "soul-spirit" state, but I hesitate to use the term *spirit* here because it could be confused with apparitions or spiritism.) The soulish state describes the present condition of the dead. We have already noted that it was described by our Lord in Luke 16:19-31 as a condition of life that is quite different from that of our physical life. In this state we are conscious and recognizable, and we can converse and be comforted or tormented. We will remember earthly events, and those who go to torment may not pass over into comfort. The Old Testament believers, as we have seen, have been taken by Christ up into Paradise, where they have already been joined by the souls of Christians ever since the first century. Also, the soulish state is attained immediately upon death.

No Limbo or Purgatory

The soulish state should not be confused with purgatory or limbo, which are not found in the Word of God, but were conceived by the imagination of man. Purgatory is said to be a place where men go to do penance or suffer for the sins they have committed in this world in order to purify them for a better afterlife. The startling difference between the biblical presentation of the present state of the dead and this false teaching is that there is no indication whatever in the Bible that those in the torment section of Sheol-Hades or those in heaven will ever be anywhere but where they are for all eternity. We have already learned that anyone who goes to the place of torment can never bridge the great gulf fixed and enter Paradise. On the contrary, all those who are presently in torment will eventually be cast into the lake of fire.

The suggestion that those in torment today will be granted a later opportunity to be saved contradicts Isaiah 38:18, which says, "Sheol cannot thank You, death cannot praise You; those who go down to the pit cannot hope for Your truth." The place of torment is essentially a place of suffering and is void of the teaching of truth. Therefore those who enter that place cannot hope for escape. This is a tragic truth, and we cannot diminish its reality in any way.

The Way to Hades

The way to Hades is the way of neglect. The Bible tells us, "How shall we escape if we neglect so great a salvation?" (Hebrews 2:3). A person winds up in Hades not simply because he is rich or poor, or because he is a murderer, a whoremonger, or a thief. A man is sent to Hades because he is an *unbeliever*—because he has never accepted Jesus Christ as his own Savior. According to John 3:18, "He who believes in Him is not condemned; but he who does not believe is condemned already, because he has not believed in the name of the only begotten Son of God."

Note that both those who go to Paradise and those who end up in Hades are sinners. The latter die in their sins, while those who reside in Paradise were forgiven of their sins sometime during their earthly life. Jesus Himself gave us clear directions on how to obtain admittance to this glorious place when He said, "I am the way, the truth, and the life. No one comes to the Father except through Me" (John 14:6). Only by Jesus Christ can we gain access to the Father. Inasmuch as the Father is in heaven (where Paradise is located), it follows that only by Jesus Christ do we have access to heaven. All of us deserve to go to hell (Romans 3:23; 6:23), and only through faith in the Lord Jesus Christ and His finished work on Calvary's cross can we escape Hades and hell. John 1:12 says, "As many as received Him, to them He gave the right to become children of God, even to those that believe in His name."

The Message of Sheol

The message of Sheol-Hades can be put into one word—a word found in Luke 16:30. The rich man in Hades pleaded with Abraham to send Lazarus back to life to warn the rich man's five brethren. What was it that the rich man anxiously wished Lazarus to tell his brothers to do? *Repent.* He said, "If one goes to them from the dead, they will repent."

If it were possible for a departed soul to return from Hades to give one last message to his living loved ones, it would be the same message that the rich man wanted to give to his brothers— REPENT so that you might avoid this awful place. The greatest tragedy in the world is not that Jesus Christ was crucified on the cross, but that men and women have heard the message that Christ died to save them from Hades and hell but have rejected it, refusing to repent and believe on Him. In spite of the fact that Christ has died for them, they will spend eternity in torment. To activate the eternal effects of God's forgiveness of sins through the death of His Son, a person must call on the name of the Lord and be saved (Romans 10:13). There is no other way—and no second chance.

17

THE GREAT
WHITE THRONE JUDGMENT

Written intuitively on the table of every man's heart is the knowledge that one day he will be ushered into God's presence in order to give an account of himself. One of the reasons that many agnostics, humanists, and unbelievers refuse to acknowledge the existence of God is that they are subconsciously afraid of one day facing Him at the judgment. Unfortunately for them, disbelief does not negate the fact of judgment, for the Bible is abundantly clear that after death comes judgment: "It is appointed for men to die once, but after this the judgment" (Hebrews 9:27).

The fact of judgment in the afterlife is not a teaching unique to New Testament Christianity; it was taught clearly in the Old Testament. The most frequent mention of this event came from the lips of Jesus Christ, who one day will be the Judge before whom men and women will stand (John 5:22). For a sample of our Lord's teaching on this subject, see Matthew 13:37-43. We also find a graphic description of that ultimate judgment day in Revelation 20:11-15, which describes the Great White Throne Judgment. It is awesome to contemplate!

~ ~ ~

The Great White Throne Judgment

Read Revelation 20:11-15 carefully.
Describe "the dead" of verse 12. (See also 1 Timothy 5:6.)

Name the two kinds of books mentioned in verse 12.

Why are the books of "works" used (verse 13)?

Where do these people come from?

Describe the "second death" (verse 14).

Look up the following verses and write the title ascribed to the book mentioned in that verse, and describe the book.

Psalm 69:28:

Revelation 13:8:

Exodus 32:33:

Revelation 3:5:

Revelation 21:27:

Revelation 22:19:

Are these books different? In what ways(s)?

What keeps a person from being cast into the lake of fire (Revelation 20:15)?

The following scriptures give us information about the lake of fire. Read the verses and describe this place.

Revelation 20:14,15:

Revelation 21:8:

Mark 9:43:

≈ ≈ ≈

The Time of This Judgment

The Great White Throne Judgment occurs at the end of the millennial kingdom, after Satan has led his insurrection but failed. At the time of this judgment, Satan, the beast, and the False Prophet have already been thrown into the lake of fire. Looking at Figure 16 in the previous chapter, you'll notice this judgment is located at the extreme end of the time line, just before the beginning of the ages to come. These ages are called "the new heaven and the new earth" and are predicted in Revelation chapters 21 and 22. The last event, then, before we enter into the heaven that Jesus promised to prepare, is the Great White Throne Judgment.

On a flight from Salt Lake City to San Francisco I was seated next to a salesman who claimed he had never read a Bible. The closest he had ever been to a church was to drop off his daughter every other week for Sunday school on his way to the golf course. I asked him if he would submit to an experiment, to which he agreed. Many people say the Bible is a difficult book to understand, particularly the book of Revelation. Turning to Revelation 20:11-15, I handed him my Bible with only this brief instruction: "This is a prophecy about a future event." I waited as he read. His cheerful mood changed abruptly, and soon he exclaimed, "If that's true, I'd better get right with God!"

That salesman put into words the main reason God has given us so much information about the afterlife judgment that awaits all those who reject or neglect God. He does not want people to face eternity in hell. He longs for people to become saved and live with Him forever in heaven.

We have already seen in Acts 17:30,31 that God will judge the world by "the Man whom He has ordained." We may well ask, whom has He ordained? The answer appears in the latter part of the verse: whom He has raised "from the dead." The Lord Jesus Christ is the only Person in world history who can match this description. He is the only One who could judge the world "in righteousness," for only He is "without sin" (1 Peter 2:22).

John 5:22 confirms Christ's identity as the Judge; Jesus said "The Father judges no one, but has committed all judgment to the Son." Therefore we come to the irrefutable conclusion that the Judge who sits on the Great White Throne is none other than the Lord Jesus Christ Himself. The very Person who was rejected and scorned by men will ultimately sit in judgment on them. That is a very sobering thought!

Also, keep in mind that Christ, even when He was on this earth in His human body, had the incredible ability to look at a person and know him intimately. You can be sure no individual will be able to hide himself from the Savior's penetrating eyes on judgment day! As the Bible says, "There is no creature hidden from His sight, but all things are naked and open to the eyes of Him to whom we must give account" (Hebrews 4:13). We also read, "There is nothing covered that will not be revealed, and hidden that will not be known" (Matthew 10:26).

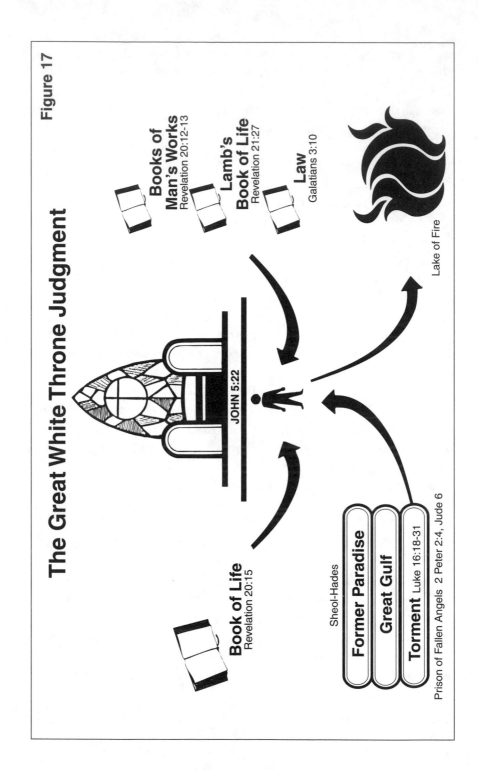

Figure 17

The Great White Throne Judgment

Books of Man's Works Revelation 20:12-13

Lamb's Book of Life Revelation 21:27

Law Galatians 3:10

JOHN 5:22

Book of Life Revelation 20:15

Lake of Fire

Sheol-Hades

Former Paradise

Great Gulf

Torment Luke 16:18-31

Prison of Fallen Angels 2 Peter 2:4, Jude 6

The Participants at This Judgment

Now that we have verified the identity of the Judge, let's consider the identity of those to be judged. John reports in Revelation 20:12, "I saw the dead, small and great, standing before God." It is significant to note that all those who stand at the Great White Throne Judgment are "the dead"—dead in trespasses and sins because of their rejection of Jesus Christ. Note that the dead are referred to as "small and great." God, who is no respecter of persons, judges fairly without regard to intellectual, physical, financial, or positional status.

Whether the remains or ashes of the dead are in the grave, in a mausoleum, on the earth, or in the sea, God will resurrect His creatures to their original bodies, souls, and spirits. These remains will be resurrected and united with their souls and spirits as they come up out of the place of torment, and in this resurrected form they will stand before the throne.

The Various Books of Judgment

"And books were opened....And the dead were judged according to their works, by the things which were written in the books" (Revelation 20:12). Evidently God owns a complete set of books that records every thought, motive, and action of a person's life, waiting to be recalled on judgment day. It may be that each of us has an angel who, in this life, is responsible for recording everything we do. In connection with this thought, it is well to consider Ecclesiastes 12:14: "God will bring every work into judgment, including every secret thing, whether it is good or whether it is evil." In this final hour, the books of man's works (his deeds) will be opened.

Degrees of Punishment

Isaiah 45:21 tells us that God is a just God, and Hebrews 2:2 advises us that "every transgression and disobedience" will receive "a just reward." Because God is just, we can be certain that He will not treat the heathen—those who have never heard the gospel of Jesus Christ—with the same judgment as the person who has listened to the message before and rejected it. Neither will He recompense the so-called "moral citizen" (doctor, teacher, good neighbor) who has lived a comparatively decent life (though still short of the standard of God) in exactly the same way as He will Adolf Hitler, under whose regime six million of God's chosen people were slain.

Matthew 11:21-24 shows us that those with extensive opportunities to receive the truth yet reject it are subject to greater condemnation than those who have never heard the truth. The cities mentioned—cities in which Christ did many of his mighty works—were compared to the wicked cities of Sodom, Gomorrah, Tyre, and Sidon. The residents of the cities that heard Christ yet rejected Him will be much more severely judged than those who didn't have such an opportunity. For Jesus to say, "It will be more tolerable for Tyre and Sidon in the day of judgment" than for Chorazin, where Christ taught and performed many miracles, establishes the fact that those who have heard the gospel and rejected it will fall into greater judgment than the homosexual sinners in Sodom.

It is imperative that every unbeliever recognize the truth that the Lord Jesus Christ will hold him accountable in proportion to the degree of opportunity he has had. The gospel of Jesus Christ is preached in almost every city and is available by radio, television, or printed page to almost everyone in the Western world. The "recording angels" know and record all the times that the gospel has been heard by people.

To be sure, no part of hell will be a desirable place, for it is all a place of torment. But the suffering of the heathen who have never heard the gospel will not be the same as that of people who have rejected God's "so great a salvation."

The Books of Life

Now it is time to examine the two books that await every person's encounter with God. Although they are similar, they bear significant differences that distinguish them from one another.

The New Testament refers to the Book of Life eight different times, and although the Old Testament does not call it by that name, it does allude three times to a book in which names are written. The psalmist speaks of the righteous as having their names written in "the book of the living" (Psalm 69:28 KJV), so it is a book in which righteous people have their names written.

Revelation 13:8 tells us about the other Book of Life—"the book of life of the Lamb." The Lamb is without doubt the Lord Jesus Christ, for only He is the "Lamb of God who takes away the sin of the world" (John 1:29). Because Christ came into the world to save sinners and to give them eternal life, the Lamb's Book of Life is the book of Jesus Christ in which are entered the names of those who have received His eternal life. (I am inclined to believe that this is a book in which only the believers who have lived since the cross have their names written.)

The above-mentioned verse indicates that during the Tribulation, those whose names are not written in the Lamb's book will worship the Antichrist. During that period, all people will bear a mark. The worshipers of the Antichrist, those who have rejected the Savior, will carry the mark of the Beast (Revelation 13:16). Those who have turned to Christ will feature a mark that is the Lamb's Father's "name written on their foreheads" (Revelation 14:1). The believers in Revelation 13:8 do not worship the Beast because their names are written in the book of the Lamb. Revelation 21:27 tells us that the only people who will enter into the Holy City are "those who are written in the Lamb's Book of Life." A person's eternal destiny, then, is based on whether or not his name is written in the Lamb's Book of Life!

The major difference between the two books we've discussed is that the Book of Life seems to contain the names of *all living people*, whereas the Lamb's Book of Life includes only the names of those who call upon the Lamb for salvation. A second difference is that the Book of Life is referred to as God the Father's book in Exodus 32:33; it records all those whom God the Creator has made. It is, then, the book of the living, much like the records book at the local county government office. On the other hand, the Lamb's Book of Life is referred to as God the Son's book (Revelation 13:8). We may conclude, then, that this book contains the names of all those who have received the new life that the Son provides.

The third and most important difference between these books is that a person may have his name blotted out of the Book of Life, but not out of the Lamb's Book of Life. In Exodus 32:33, the Lord said to Moses, "Whoever has sinned against Me, I will blot him out of My book." It is possible, therefore, to have one's name erased from the Book of Life because of sin.

The Lamb's Book of Life is different, however. Revelation 3:5 promises, "He who overcomes shall be clothed in white garments, and I will *not blot out* his name from the Book of Life." An overcomer is a believer who is clothed in the white garments of Christ; the Creator has imputed to him divine righteousness, and his name cannot be blotted out of the Lamb's Book of Life.

Primarily because a person's name *can* be blotted out of the Book of Life, I am convinced that the Book of Life and the Lamb's Book of Life are not the same book. As we have seen, the Lamb's book contains the names of all those who have been born again through the shed blood of the Lamb, which is the guarantee that we have eternal life. Therefore we can be sure that these are two distinctly separate books. The Book of Life is that book in which the names of all people ever born into the world are written. If, at the time of a person's death, he has not called upon the Lord Jesus Christ for salvation, his name is blotted out of the Book of Life. If he *has* accepted Christ and His forgiveness of sins, his name is indelibly recorded in the Lamb's Book of Life, and entrance into the Holy City is guaranteed (Revelation 21:27).

God's Double-Check

We have spent some time discussing the Book of Life, but in order to grasp its full importance we need to look at Revelation 20:15: "Anyone not found written in the Book of Life was cast into the lake of fire." In a sense, this is God's double-check at the Great White Throne Judgment. As a person comes forward, he is judged by the book of the law, by the books of his works, and by the Lamb's Book of Life. Then, just before he receives his sentence, he is given a double-check. The recording angel will refer to the book, and anyone not found written in the Book of Life will be thrown into the lake of fire. This is consistent with the fact that the Bible repeatedly contrasts two kinds of people on earth, using such words as "believing" and "unbelieving," "saved" and "unsaved," "condemned" and "not condemned," "righteous" and "unrighteous," "just" and "unjust."

This contrast is maintained in the fact that people's names are either written or not written in the Book of Life. In that hour of judgment there will be no hesitation or question, for a person's name is either written or not written—it must be one way or the other.

The Book of Life contains the names of all living souls—as though a loving God wants all people to be saved and anticipates their salvation by writing their names into the Book of Life. But to *keep* your name there, you must have your name written in the Lamb's Book of Life as a result of receiving the Lamb as your Lord and Savior.

One Last Event

There is an awesome scene recorded in Philippians that is rarely mentioned in this relation to future judgment, but it should be. The apostle Paul wrote this about Jesus:

> Therefore God...also has highly exalted Him and given Him the name which is above every name, that at the name of Jesus every knee should bow, of those in heaven, and of those on earth, and of those under the earth, and that every tongue should confess that Jesus Christ is Lord, to the glory of God the Father (Philippians 2:9-11).

After giving a wonderful description of how Christ was willing to humble Himself and become "obedient to the point of death, even the death of the cross" (verse 8) Paul warns that there is a day coming when "every knee should bow, and every tongue confess that Jesus Christ is Lord" (verse 10). All the skeptics, infidels, procrastinators, and rejecters of Christ will acknowledge that Jesus Christ is Lord! It won't be believers alone who bow and acknowledge Christ as Lord.

Since all men will one day bend their knee to Jesus Christ—and this will probably happen at the close of the Great White Throne Judgment—it makes sense that it is far better to acknowledge Christ as Lord now, voluntarily, rather than to reject Him in this life and wait to be forced to do so that day and then be cast into the lake of fire.

Why Was Hell Created?

Did you know that hell was created for a specific purpose? That purpose is found in Matthew 25:41: "Then He will also say to those on the left hand, 'Depart from Me, you cursed, into the everlasting fire prepared for the devil and his angels.'" This statement made by Jesus Christ, relating to judgment day, points out that hell was created for the judgment of the devil and his angels. The apostle Peter sheds more light on this with these words in 2 Peter 2:4: "If God did not spare the angels who sinned, but cast them down to hell and delivered them into chains of darkness, to be reserved for judgment...." Because the angels sinned, they are being "reserved for judgment."

Just when these angels sinned with the devil is not absolutely clear. In the book of Job we learn that the angels were present at the creation of the earth. It suggests that the earth was the choice dwelling place of the angels for perhaps many years, and then Lucifer—the greatest created being, perfect in all his ways in the day he was made—rebelled against God (Ezekiel 28:15; Isaiah 14:12-15). It is impressive to notice the number of angels that fell on that fateful day. Revelation 12:4 tells us, "His tail drew a third of the stars of heaven and threw them to the earth." Think of it—one-third of the angels chose to rebel against the most high God and to follow Lucifer, the great deceiver!

These statements from the Lord Jesus Christ and the apostle Peter, seem to indicate that the lake of fire was not originally intended for man at all, but for the eternal punishment of supernatural beings like the devil and his angels. From the book of Revelation, particularly in 20:11-15, we see that unsaved people will be cast into the lake of fire in spite of the fact that it was not originally created for them. There they will endure indescribable misery and suffering, and be numbered among the hosts of fallen supernatural beings.

Why People Go to Hell

People are sent to hell only if they are not fit to enter heaven. The Lord Jesus Christ said in John 3:3, "Most assuredly, I say to you, unless one is born again, he cannot see the kingdom of God." "Born again" means "born from above" or "born anew," indicating that natural, physical birth is not sufficient to entitle a person to see the kingdom of God. Unless a person is born again, he or she is unprepared for the spiritual delights of heaven; he or she must spend eternity in the lake of fire. The apostle Paul made this clear in 1 Corinthians 15:50: "Flesh and blood cannot inherit the kingdom of God; nor does corruption inherit incorruption." Our corrupt mortal bodies cannot dwell in heaven without contaminating it, for heaven is a perfect place.

A Christian, then, has full assurance that he is going to heaven not because he is naturally fit for heaven, but because he has been made fit by the new birth through Jesus Christ. This is not true for the ungodly person, who is "dead" toward God even though he is alive physically. Consequently he can respond only to the resurrection of the dead, which leads to the second death.

The Savior Is Waiting

If Jesus Christ had not come into this world to die for our sins, we would all be sent to hell. None of us is good enough for heaven. But because He loves us, Jesus paid the penalty and accepted total punishment for all our offenses against Him, thereby making heaven available to us. It is not that our sins are somehow minimized or overlooked; they are completely forgiven and Christ's righteousness is imputed to us. Those who are foolish enough to pass up this free ticket to heaven are reserving for themselves a spot in hell.

In the archives of the Supreme Court of the United States is the record of a very strange incident that took place during the term of President Andrew Jackson. A man named George Wilson was sentenced to die by hanging for a crime he had committed. Somehow the story came before the president, who granted Wilson a pardon. To everyone's amazement, Wilson tore the pardon to shreds and threw it on the floor of his prison cell. The ensuing legal argument concerned the validity of a pardon that was refused, and the question arose as to whether or not Wilson should be freed or hanged. After great deliberation, the U.S. Supreme Court ruled as follows: "A pardon is a writing, the value of which is dependent upon the acceptance by the individual for whom it is intended." It was therefore decreed by the court that George Wilson be hanged until dead—not because a pardon was not offered, but because it was not accepted.

This is a perfect picture of the sinner who hears the gospel of Jesus Christ and knows that God has written a pardon for him, yet rejects Him and thus forfeits his right to the pardon. If you are without the Savior today, it is because you choose to be. Your choice to reject Jesus Christ automatically invalidates your pardon and sentences you to the lake of fire.

During this life, all of us are confronted with a choice. We can admit we are sinners in need of a Savior and invite Jesus Christ into our lives as Lord and Savior, or we can reject Him. Where we live in eternity will be determined by that choice. Those who have chosen to put their faith in Christ will rule and reign with Him during the 1,000-year kingdom and then go on into the eternal ages with Him forever. Those who reject Him will be "cast into the lake of fire" (Revelation 20:15).

It is with that in mind that the apostle Paul warned: "Behold, now is the accepted time; behold, now is the day of salvation" (2 Corinthians 6:2).

The Lake of Fire

Those who do not have their name written in the Lamb's Book of Life (which guarantees that their name remains in the Book of Life) will, according to Revelation 20:15, be "cast into the lake of fire," the final dwelling place of the unbelieving dead. It is the hell that Revelation 20:14 calls "the second death." Sinners die once, are kept in torment until the end of the 1,000 years, and are then resurrected to the Great White Throne Judgment, where the Christ they refused to accept as Savior determines the degree or intensity of their eternal punishment. He then will banish them to the lake of fire—for eternity.

This will not be a pretty sight—nor is it necessary, either! For the Bible says, "Believe on the Lord Jesus Christ, and you *will* be saved" (Acts 16:31, emphasis added).

One of the clearest offers of salvation in all the Bible came from our Lord Jesus Christ Himself:

> Most assuredly, I say to you, he who hears My word and believes in Him who sent Me has everlasting life, and shall not come into judgment, but has passed from death into life (John 5:24).

Make that right choice today!

DRAWING NEARER TO
CHRIST'S RETURN

I t is absolutely incredible how much the world scene continues to change all around us. The political turmoil in the Middle East, regions of the former Soviet Union, and elsewhere shows no signs of lessening. The United Nations (U.N.), for lack of strong leadership, is still so inept that it is said there are more than 50 wars or revolutions going on in the world right now. And even though the U.N. has celebrated the fiftieth anniversary of its historical attempt to bring peace to the world, the fact is that we have had more wars during those 50 years than at any comparable period in world history.

What many people don't realize is just how ripe world conditions are for the end times. All we lack is a powerfully clever individual with a Roman ancestry, who can arise and, by promising *peace* to a war-weary world, take control of the powerful U.N. (or an agency like it) and rule the world—just like the Bible predicts for the last days!

In addition, the weather phenomenons predicted by Jesus Christ and His prophets have struck with a vengeance. Earthquakes have occurred at unprecedented levels. The U.S. Geological Department has reported that our globe experienced a record number of killer earthquakes through the 1980s. From 1950 through 1989, each decade exceeded the decade before in the total number and intensity of catastrophic earthquakes. Now it is revealed that the first five years of the 1990s have exceeded the 1980s, and 1996 exceeded any other year and had almost as many as the first five years of the 1990s combined! Only a fool would deny that, as we approach the next millennium, the earth is twisting and moving in anticipation of *the big one* that Hollywood sensationalizes and, more importantly, the Bible predicts. In fact, the Bible predicts two giant earthquakes yet to come!

In America we have experienced unprecedented snows and hurricanes in the east; record-breaking floods, tornadoes, and hurricanes in the central states; and unprecedented earthquakes, fires, and rains in the west. Something catastrophic is going on! But it isn't just in America—it is worldwide. So much so that insurance companies fear the possibility of bankruptcy because of having to pay so much for disaster damages all over the earth.

In addition, sexually transmitted diseases have gotten much worse, and there's still no cure for AIDS despite the billions of dollars invested in research. The Ebola plague, so much like some of those predicted in the book of Revelation for the last days, has terrified even some of our best scientists.

And, of course, there's the proliferation of nuclear arms and chemical weaponry that is terrifying. The world is vulnerable to rogue nations like Iran, Libya, and China, none of which would hesitate to use or threaten to use nuclear weapons to impose their despotic will. And even worse is the threat of terrorists getting such devices that, in this day of computer miniaturizations, can be delivered in a briefcase!

Who can truly look forward to a safe and fulfilling future? Only the Christian who has made his personal peace with God through His Son Jesus Christ. And even then such an individual needs to study the prophetic word of God so as not to be confused by the many false teachers that have arisen in these last days.

One of the most significant warnings our Lord gave in His teachings about the last days is this: "Take heed that no one deceives you. For many will come in My name, saying, 'I am the Christ,' and will deceive many" (Matthew 24:4,5). Later, in verse 11, Jesus states, "Many false prophets will rise up and deceive many." And still later in verses 24,25 He says, "False Christs and false prophets will rise and show great signs and wonders so as to deceive, if possible, even the elect. See, I have told you beforehand."

Our Lord knew that in the last days, false teachings would run rampant. Daniel, Peter, and Paul also warned of deceivers. The church has always been plagued by false teachers, for the devil is, as Jesus said, the master deceiver. Who can deny that false teachers are arising in unprecedented numbers today? These are just some of the catalysts that have spurred a rapidly growing interest in prophecy books, cassettes, videos, and movies. My own long-standing dream of writing a prophetic novel to accurately present the Bible truths of future events has gone off the charts. Written with Jerry Jenkins, *Left Behind* became the number-one selling Christian fiction book in 1996. The subsequent books in the series have all gone on to become bestsellers and, more importantly, compelled many people to receive Christ as their Savior.

I pray that upon completing this book, you will continue to study Bible prophecy for yourself to see what really is coming to pass. Historically, whenever Christians have studied prophecy they have become excited about the Lord's soon return, which has produced three powerful results: 1) a desire for holy living in an unholy age; 2) a new zeal for evangelism and soul-winning; 3) a renewed interest in world missions that produces more praying, giving, and going into all the world to preach the gospel. Our Lord said, "This gospel of the kingdom will be preached in all the world as a witness to all nations, and *then the end will come*" (Matthew 24:14, emphasis added).

As you continue to study Bible prophecy, I pray you will see these results appear in your own life. And, your diligence in the study of prophecy will not only keep you from being deceived by the false prophets of our day, but it will warm your heart and cause you to "lift up your [heads], because your redemption draws near" (Luke 21:28). You will find yourself waking up each morning saying in your heart, "Perhaps today my Lord will come!"

ABOUT THE AUTHOR

Tim LaHaye is the bestselling author of more than 40 books, some of which have been translated into 32 languages, with more than ten million copies in print. He is a popular prophecy conference and family life speaker. His other prophecy books include *Are We Living in the End Times?*, *Revelation Unveiled*, and *Charting the End Times*. His unique prophetic Left Behind series, written with Jerry Jenkins, became an instant bestseller. It includes *Left Behind*, *Tribulation Force*, *Nicolae*, *Soul Harvest*, *Apollyon*, *Assassins*, *The Indwelling*, *The Mark*, *Desecration*, and five more books to come.

Some of his other popular books have been written with his wife, Beverly, the founder of Concerned Women for America, the largest women's organization in the nation. These include *The Act of Marriage* and *The Spirit-Controlled Family*.

NOTE TO BIBLE TEACHERS

This book lends itself nicely to small group Bible classes for Sunday school, or in homes. Beautiful transparencies of the charts in this book* can be ordered for a reasonable fee from:

Visualize-It Productions
4263 Alta Mira Drive
La Mesa, CA 92041
(619) 670-1894 or 660-6172

*As indicated in the text, a few of the charts are derived from sources other than Visualize-It Productions. These charts are not available as transparencies.

OTHER HARVEST HOUSE BOOKS
by Tim and Beverly LaHaye

CHARTING THE END TIMES
Tim LaHaye and Thomas Ice

A unique book that provides more than 50 full-color charts to help give a comprehensive idea of what will happen during the last days. Includes a master foldout chart portraying God's complete plan for the ages.

I LOVE YOU, BUT WHY ARE WE SO DIFFERENT?
Tim LaHaye

Help in understanding *why* opposites attract and how opposite temperaments can enrich both partners, resulting in an incredibly dynamic relationship. Includes biblical principles that will send marriages soaring to new heights.

THE SPIRIT-CONTROLLED WOMAN
Beverly LaHaye

This bestseller gives the Christian woman practical help in understanding herself and the weaknesses she encounters in her private life and in her relationships. Covers every stage of a woman's life.

UNDERSTANDING YOUR CHILD'S TEMPERAMENT
Beverly LaHaye

Answers to some of the frustrating problems parents face. Includes proven concepts that will help you to relate to your children on a one-to-one basis and train each child according to his or her unique temperament.

A DIFFERENT KIND OF STRENGTH
Beverly LaHaye and Janice Shaw Crouse

Throughout history, women have played vital, sometimes surprising roles in God's incredible plans. In Matthew's Gospel, we find five such women in Christ's lineage—Tamar, Rahab, Ruth, Bathsheba, and Mary. Through God's grace and power, each woman left an inspiring legacy of courage and strength—a legacy any woman can make her own today.

HOW TO STUDY THE BIBLE FOR YOURSELF

(Harvest House Publishers)

BY TIM LAHAYE

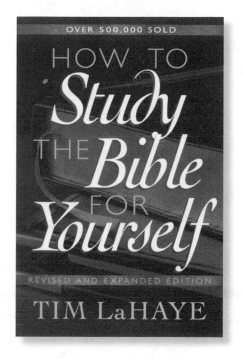

This excellent book already has over 500,000 copies in print. It provides fascinating study helps and charts that will make personal Bible study more interesting and exciting. A three-year program is outlined for a good working knowledge of the Bible. Using this book can produce maturity in your Christian life in a relatively short period of time.

These unique techniques work for people in groups of 15 to 100 as well as on a one-on-one basis.

Available at your local Christian bookstore.